Who Patrols the Streets?

Who Patrols the Streets?

An International Comparative Study of Plural Policing

Jan Terpstra
Bas van Stokkom
Ruben Spreeuwers

eleven
international publishing

Published, sold and distributed by Eleven International Publishing
P.O. Box 85576
2508 CG The Hague
The Netherlands
Tel.: +31 70 33 070 33
Fax: +31 70 33 070 30
e-mail: sales@budh.nl
www.elevenpub.com

Sold and distributed in USA and Canada
International Specialized Book Services
920 NE 58th Avenue, Suite 300
Portland, OR 97213-3786, USA
Tel: 1-800-944-6190 (toll-free)
Fax: +1-503-280-8832
orders@isbs.com
www.isbs.com

Eleven International Publishing is an imprint of Boom uitgevers Den Haag.

ISBN 978-94-6236-079-2
ISBN 978-94-6094-826-8 (E-book)

Printed in The Netherlands

Preface

Awareness has been increasing over the past few decades that the study of policing, security and criminal justice needs an international comparative approach. To a significant degree, policing, security and criminal justice have become transnational phenomena, with international institutions that cross the boundaries of separate jurisdictions. Processes of policy transfer and imitation have increased international similarities between what were previously purely national institutions. By conducting detailed comparative studies in different national contexts, however, evidence may be found not only of similarities in policing, security, and criminal justice, but also of important differences. Too often it is assumed that the 'grand theories', as Charles Wright Mills (1959) called them, of policing and security, such as the nodal governance of security, the shift from government to governance (presumably a more neutral phrase for rolling back the state), the new punitive turn, the privatization of security, or the loss of citizens' trust in police and criminal justice institutions (to mention just a few), are more or less universal. Detailed comparative studies might help us understand whether this is really true, and prevent doom-laden scenarios from being too readily accepted as inescapable, generalized global phenomena.

Although there seems to be a fair degree of consensus on the need to conduct such international comparative research, in practice there are many obstacles that must be overcome. Many of these are related to differences in language, cultural traditions, legal systems, and political sensitivities, which may be hard to understand and overcome if one cleaves too much to the tried-and-trusted views and realities of one's own national context.

This international comparative study deals with the pluralization of policing in five different countries. For the past two decades all these countries have been confronted with a rise in new forms of policing in public and semipublic places, in addition to the regular public police. New uniformed officers are to be found in all these countries, with names, such as surveillance officer, community guard, warden, support officer or municipal patroller, that differ as much as their uniforms, equipment, legal powers, social status, relations with the public police, etc. The complexity of this field becomes even more impressive if one realizes that this pluralization of policing is largely a local phenomenon, implying significant differences from city to city, and from municipality to municipality, even within a single country. Although the pluralization processes were broadly similar in all these countries, with more or less comparable factors contributing to the rise and differentiation of local policing, the huge differences between the countries are even more obvious. In this book we have not only tried to describe an abundance of detail about local plural policing in each of these countries. To avoid the risk of an 'abstracted empiricism' (to use another term coined by Wright Mills), we have also tried to comprehend the differences and similarities in the local pluralization of policing, without falling into the trap of hasty generalizations.

This book is based on a study conducted in 2012/2013, commissioned and funded by the Research and Documentation Centre (WODC) of the Ministry of Security and Justice of the Netherlands. A Dutch-language report of this study can be downloaded from the WODC website. Although this book has a broader focus, in many respects it is based upon this report.

We are very grateful to the many persons whom we were able to interview in the five different countries. We also want to thank the members of the advisory commission that was established by the WODC for this study, who commented on the draft chapters of the Dutch report and provided us with several suggestions for improvement.
We would also like to thank several persons who read parts of our book and prevented us from making all kinds of mistakes in our understanding of legal complexities and specific national situations: Ted Carroll, Rian de Jong, Elke Devroe, Trevor Jones, and Gregor Wenda. Teun Eikenaar supported us with information about the situation in the Netherlands. We are not native English writers, which means that we have been very dependent on our editor Ian Priestnall, who often operates only behind the scenes. We would like to thank him for all his efforts to make our texts acceptable and understandable to an international audience. Of course, any errors or imprecision that remain in the book can only be seen as our own responsibility.

Jan Terpstra, Bas van Stokkom & Ruben Spreeuwers

Table of contents

1 Pluralization of policing: introduction

In many countries over the past twenty years or so – apparently almost all over the world – a new division of responsibilities has arisen in the management of crime and disorder. Public security is no longer considered to be the task of the police alone. Other agencies, both public and private, have increasingly become involved in preventing and combating nuisance, social disorder and crime.
Since the early 1990s patrolling, guardianship and the enforcement of law and order have no longer been defined as the exclusive task of the police. (This, of course, always was a myth, but is now more clearly recognized as such: Jones & Newburn, 2002; Zedner, 2006.) In addition to the regular public police there are now all kinds of (non-police) guards, patrollers, wardens and officers working in the public space, under the eyes of the general public. What has arisen in a period of only two decades is a complex of bodies and agencies for guarding, surveillance and enforcement tasks, both in the public domain (on the streets, the market or in the parks), and in areas that are privately owned but are perceived by many citizens as public and freely accessible (often called the semipublic space), such as large malls, entertainment areas or business parks.
In this new security complex (Terpstra, 2010a) both public and private workers and officers are used. They can provide their services by order of both public and private institutions (Bayley & Shearing, 2001). There are numerous examples of these new patrollers, guards, wardens and officers. They operate under different titles, varying not only from jurisdiction to jurisdiction, but often also from city to city, and even according to location and organization. In addition, there are also important differences in the legal basis underlying these new workers and officers, their specific tasks, their (formal) powers, their equipment and uniform, etc. It seems likely that most citizens will find this new complex of policing bodies opaque, difficult to see through. Most citizens probably do not understand the differences between all these people in uniform, what their powers and mandate actually are, and in what respect they differ (or not) from the regular or 'ordinary' police.

This change in security and the rise of these new wardens, guardians and enforcement workers who deliver surveillance and enforcement services in the public space, has been described in several ways in the international scientific literature.

It has often been analysed as the rise of *plural policing* (Loader, 2000; Crawford, Lister, Blackburn and Burnett, 2005; Jones & Newburn, 2006c). During the high days of the modern police force, the concepts of *police* and *policing* were seen as almost identical. Now these terms increasingly refer to phenomena that only partially overlap (Loader, 2000; Crawford, 2003). Policing (or police work in its broadest sense) can increasingly be found in other organizations than the regular police force. The outcome of these developments may also be described in other ways, such as the rise of a police complex (Hoogenboom, 1994) or of a 'police extended family' (Johnston, 2003 and 2005).
These developments have not only produced a highly confused, opaque landscape of guards, surveillance workers, patrollers and enforcement officers in the public and semipublic space, they also raise a number of important questions that refer to very different issues. What are the circumstances that have contributed to this pluralization of policing? What are the tasks of these new professionals? What are their (formal) powers and what is the legal basis of their work? To what extent are they supervised and held accountable for their work? What is their relationship with the regular police and is there some form of cooperation with the police? To what extent and how are the rights of citizens protected from interventions by these workers? These questions relate not only to formal regulations and procedures, but also to the ways these are implemented in practice.

The developments roughly outlined above can be found in many jurisdictions, not only in Europe but also in other parts of the world. One of the few available international reviews in this area was published by Jones and Newburn (2006c). Their book shows that in addition to some broad similarities, there are significant differences in the pluralization of policing between jurisdictions. Given the differences in this process of pluralization it may be expected that the countries were confronted with different problems and that different political, organizational and practical questions were raised. For that reason it is relevant to look beyond national borders to learn about developments elsewhere, about the kinds of strategy used to cope with these problems, and how these questions were answered.

In the following chapters we present the main findings and conclusions of an international comparative study on the pluralization of policing in a number of countries: the Netherlands, England & Wales, Austria, Belgium, and Canada. For each of these countries we describe the new forms of policing that have arisen in the public or semipublic public space, in addition to the regular police, and the circumstances that contributed to this pluralization. What are the tasks and powers of these new policing officers? What is their position in relation to the regular police? What kinds of problem are raised by these new pluralized forms of policing? What kinds of strategy are used to address these problems in the different countries? What are the main differences and similarities in plural policing between these countries, and how can these be understood?

This chapter presents the research questions and the design and methods of this study. First, however, we present a brief review of factors and circumstances that have contributed to the rise of these new auxiliary policing bodies over the past two decades. This section is based on the available international literature in the field (1.1). The research questions are dealt with next (1.2), as well as the design and research methods of the study (1.3). Finally, the general outline of the book is presented (1.4).

1.1 Background

The rise of new patrollers, wardens, guards and enforcement officers in the public space, who are not an element of the regular police, can be seen as resulting from a complex of interrelated social, political and economic circumstances and changes (Bayley & Shearing, 2001; Crawford, 2003 and 2006b; Crawford & Lister, 2006; Jones & Newburn, 1999 and 2006c; Jones, Van Steden & Boutellier, 2009; Van Steden, 2007; Terpstra & Kouwenhoven, 2004; Terpstra, 2010a). Here we can give only a brief sketch of some of the main factors and circumstances.

One factor that contributed to the rise of these new guards, wardens and enforcement officers in the public space, and to the growth in their numbers, is that from about the early 1990s, large numbers of citizens in many countries had strong feelings of insecurity and were worried about public safety. Many studies showed that these feelings of insecurity and anxiety were only partially the result of high levels of objective risk. General feelings of uneasiness and ontological insecurity (Giddens, 1991) seemed to be as important as the level of objective risks and dangers. Nevertheless, for the last ten to twenty years large numbers of citizens in many Western countries have been calling on their governments to implement strong, drastic, tangible measures against crime and disorder. They commonly ask for the visible presence of a growing number of uniformed officers on the streets, viewing that as a reassuring factor. As security and crime issues have come to occupy a more important place on the political agenda, governments in many countries have appeared to be more inclined to meet such demands.

With the increasing demands for police and police work it has become clearer that there are limits to the capacities of the police, despite the fact that the numbers of police officers have been growing in many Western countries since the early 1990s, in many cases considerably (Haagsma, Smits, Waarsing & Wiebrens, 2012: 45). As a consequence, over the past two decades there has been pressure on the police in several countries to concentrate on their so-called core business or core tasks. This has happened, for instance, in Belgium (Ponsaers, Enhus &

Hutsebaut, 2006), the Netherlands (Terpstra, Van Stokkom & Gunther Moor, 2010) and England & Wales (Mawby, 2000). This is also one of the main arguments governments use to persuade other agencies to take greater responsibility for the management of crime and disorder. In several European countries (such as Belgium and the Netherlands) local governments especially acquired a central position in local security policies, and in the organization and implementation of surveillance and enforcement tasks in the public space. In several countries during those same years, policies inspired by New Public Management contributed not only to the concentration on core-business tasks, but also to the creeping centralization of the police. In such countries this has resulted in a growing distance between the police and local governments and communities, especially in rural areas (Mouhanna, 2010; Terpstra, 2004; Girling, Loader & Sparks, 2000). As a result, it is local governments in particular that are trying to find answers to the resulting deficit or gap in local policing. In some of these countries new opportunities and regulations were created at the national level (in some cases including new budgets), which local governments could use to have their own guards patrolling in the public space, with or without formal enforcement powers.

In some countries, local governments (or other public bodies at the local level) contract private security officers to do this patrolling or guardian work. This development has been enhanced by the rapid growth of private security in most developed countries for the past two to three decades, as well as an increasing level of professional competence in this kind of work (Van Steden, 2007; Van Steden & De Waard, 2013). Moreover, in many countries it is not uncommon for private agencies to contract private security officers, not only to guard their own buildings and territories, but also for patrol and surveillance in public and (especially) semipublic space like large malls, industrial areas and business parks.

The rise and growing numbers of these new public and private guards, wardens, patrollers, guardians and rule-enforcement officers are also closely related to significant changes in the urban economy and space. Public safety is perceived to have increasing economic importance in urban locations, for example as a precondition for attracting day trippers, tourists and other visitors to city centres, shopping precincts, night-life areas, places of entertainment, and large events (Van Steden, 2009). Visible surveillance and regulation of security risks are increasingly important to attract visitors, who often make their decision where to go and where to spend their money on the basis of an urban location's security image.

In many urban areas (although not to the same degree in all developed countries) there are growing numbers of so-called mass hybrid properties (Jones & Newburn, 1999; Kempa, Stenning & Wood, 2004), such as large malls, which are covered areas containing in some cases a few hundred retail stores. Although the public may perceive these areas as public space, since they appear to be freely accessible, the daily surveillance tasks are often conducted by private security officers who are contracted by the mall's private owners (alone or in association).

In some cases we may find complex forms of cooperation between public and private policing (Van Steden, 2007; Wakefield, 2003).
Finally, especially in the late 1980s and 1990s, considerations of economy and budget costs meant that all kinds of positions were disbanded and almost disappeared. People in such lines of works used to have an important secondary function of social control, like janitors, rail or bus conductors, platform guards, or wardens in apartment buildings (Newburn, 2001; Jones & Newburn, 2002). Later, when the negative consequences of this loss became visible, new positions were introduced to restore social control, now by appointing specialized wardens or contracting private security guards.

Most of the factors and circumstances described here are dealt with in the Anglo-Saxon scientific literature, especially from England & Wales, Canada, the U.S.A. and Australia. It is often not clear whether these analyses are also relevant to other jurisdictions, and if so, to what extent. With the exception of the review by Jones and Newburn (2006c) and, for example, the recent study by Donnelly (2013), there is little empirical information. As a consequence it is often not clear to what extent this pluralization of policing can also be found in other countries and what the similarities and differences are between countries. It is also often not clear whether the social, political and economic factors and circumstances mentioned here may be generalized to other countries, what their meaning is in other cultural contexts, and how they are interpreted there, and to what degree they also contributed to the pluralization of policing in other national contexts.

1.2 Research question

There are several reasons why it may be important to do international comparative research on the pluralization of policing and the rise of new wardens, guards and enforcement officers in the public space in addition to the regular police. During the past two decades many countries have undergone this pluralization process (cf. Jones & Newburn, 2006c). It is also important to get a better view of the differences in this process. Apparently similar developments may have drastically different meanings in other social and cultural contexts, which may complicate international comparative empirical research. In addition to organizational and legal differences between countries in their police system, there may also be differences in the meaning of concepts, in sensibilities, and in the actors' motivations and interests. For outsiders it may be difficult to trace these largely unwritten, informal differences and to understand them. They may refer to historical and cultural circumstances that may be almost unnoticed and taken for granted by members of a national community (Nelken, 1994 and 2002).
International comparative studies on the pluralization of policing are also important because they may shed new light on factors and circumstances that may con-

tribute to the process. Comparative studies may produce information about relevant backgrounds to this process that may be overlooked in studies that focus on one country only (Jones & Newburn, 2006a).

Finally, international comparative studies may create opportunities to learn from experience gained in other jurisdictions. Despite the differences between countries, the rise of non-police providers of policing and the de-monopolization of the police raise comparable questions and problems. It may therefore be relevant to know what strategies are being used elsewhere to cope with these problems. Examples of such questions are: What are the relations between the police and the non-police providers of policing? Who has the coordination and does the 'steering' over these new forms of policing? If private security officers are involved in surveillance and rule enforcement in public or semipublic space, how is their work regulated? How can citizens protect themselves if they object to decisions or treatment by these wardens, guards or other non-police policing officers?

These issues refer to questions that are much more fundamental than the usual considerations of practical or organizational matters or questions of effectiveness. The answers given to these underlying questions may differ between jurisdictions, because of different underlying views on policing and security as a public good (Loader & Walker, 2007). This may be related to other views on issues like the state's monopoly of violence, the (constitutional) relationship between central and local governments, the emotional and political restraints or readiness to privatize state activities and institutions, the relationship between the state and citizens, and the need for elaborate legal safeguards to protect citizens against misconduct and intrusion by uniformed (police and non-police) providers of policing and security.

In this study we focus on the pluralization of policing in a number of different countries. In each of these countries we explore and map the non-police providers of policing in the public or semipublic space, the factors that contributed to their rise and growth, what their tasks and powers are, and how these relate to those of the police. We are also interested in the question of what challenges and problems arise with this pluralization of policing. Finally: what are the similarities and differences in plural policing between these countries?

For each of the countries included in this study, we try to answer the following questions.

a. What factors and circumstances contributed to the pluralization of policing? Which non-police providers of policing are working in the public or semipublic space, and in what governmental and organisational context? What were the main arguments used to introduce these non-police providers of policing and contribute to their growth?

b. What are the tasks and (formal) powers of these non-police providers of policing and in what domains do they operate? What is the formal or legal basis of their work? Are there certain conditions and requirements to which they have to conform?
c. What are the main problems and impediments in the work and position of these non-police providers of policing? What underlying factors contribute to these problems?
d. What is the role of private security in the surveillance and enforcement in the public or semipublic space? How is this regulated?
e. What is the relationship between these non-police providers of policing and other relevant agencies, like the regular police? Is there some form of external governance of their work? Is there coordination and exchange of information between these agencies or is there a form of competition? Has there been a shift or transfer of regular police tasks to the new non-police providers of policing? Are the new non-police wardens, guards and officers identifiable as such to citizens?
f. What are the legal forms of protection that safeguard citizens against the conduct and intrusion of these non-police policing officers and workers?
g. Is there a public debate about the rise, growth and work of these non-police providers of policing in public or semipublic space? What are the main issues in these debates?

These research questions express our interest not only in formal rules and procedures, but also in the practices of these new non-police forms of patrolling, surveillance, regulation and enforcement bodies. With regard to the actual implementation of their work, however, this study is limited to some of the main outlines. We were unable to conduct extensive fieldwork in all the countries concerned.

Our study focuses on what might be called non-police (public and private) providers of policing in the public or semipublic space. That is a somewhat complex description of the professions in which we are interested. The specific groups of these policing workers differ greatly, not only from country to country, but because they are largely a local phenomenon, varying even from town to town. This implies that the terms used to describe them differ markedly, such as (if translated literally) wardens, city guards, order guardians, community guards, special investigation officers, and so on. The differences in the nature of their work, their legal basis, their formal powers, equipment, uniform, relations with the police and local government, not only make this field highly complex and difficult to penetrate; it is also often difficult to compare these groups of non-police policing workers, in some cases even within a single jurisdiction. Because all the terms used to describe these different groups of new policing professions differ so much in meaning and are often very context-dependent, we often use the native terms or, if necessary, a literal translation. By doing so we hope that the original and native context-related meaning of each of these terms is maintained as far as possible.

In this study we deal with non-police providers of policing who are mainly concerned with security and safety issues in the public or semipublic space. Some categories of non-police surveillance and enforcement officer are excluded from this study, such as guards on public transport, at railway stations, parking enforcement officers, park-keepers, or those officers charged with the enforcement of environmental protection regulations. Security and public safety are usually not the main concerns of the work of these categories of officer.

1.3 Methods and design of the study

The problem of international comparison

As was noted above, international comparative studies of police and criminal justice often raise several problems. Two different circumstances are often referred to in this context (Jones & Newburn, 2006a). Both may also be relevant to comparative studies of plural policing.

First, there is often a lack of reliable empirical data for comparison between different jurisdictions. In this study, for instance, in many countries it proved difficult to collect data about the numbers of public and private non-police policing officers working in the public or semipublic space. Most of these non-police providers of policing are local bodies, which are very dependent on local policies, decision-making, and in some cases also local sources of funding. As a result, these non-police officers and organizations may differ from place to place and in many respects. As a consequence, there is generally no overview at the national level of the numbers of such guards and officers. Often, too, there is also a comparable lack of data about citizens' views of these guards and patrolling officers, the trust they have in these officers, or the social and professional status of such officers in the public eye. As a result, it is almost impossible to give an adequate empirical international comparison of the elements of trust, legitimacy and social status of these non-police providers of policing.

Secondly, international comparative studies are faced with difficulties because of differences in (national) contexts that are often hard to fathom. In part this has to do with differences in formal rules and procedures or in legal terminology. Mostly, however, this is not the most delicate issue. These more formal contextual elements are relatively easy to detect and put into words. An example concerns the differences in the legal meaning of 'public space' in the Netherlands and Austria.[1] Unfamiliarity with this may give rise to misunderstandings about the formal role of the police in semipublic space such as mass private properties.

1 See Chapter 4 Austria.

However, for a relative outsider it may be much more difficult to understand the largely unwritten, informal context. Here we may have to do with traditions, sensitivities, emotions and hidden interests that have a strong, but mainly hidden impact in a certain national context. Differences between jurisdictions in government policy and the performance of central institutions may also be very dependent on different patterns of trust, either in reality or in imagination, between citizens and the state (Nelken, 1994). It is often even harder to find reliable information about such issues and to estimate its value. This problem has been vigorously summarized by David Nelken (2002: 180):

> 'Our guiding problem must be: how can we be sure that we are comparing 'like with like', both in terms of the distinctive elements (-) and in terms of its place in the larger culture?'

As a consequence of these methodological problems international comparative research is often confined to what Nelken (2002: 179) calls *'comparison by juxtaposition'*, a collection of more or less loose descriptions of each individual country. As a rule even such descriptions take a lot of time and energy. For this reason in practice foreign researchers are often asked to conduct the study in their own home country. This may appear the most practical way to conduct international studies, but it is probably a main reason why a common focus often remains rather vague in international comparative studies. Moreover, in many cases an actual comparison between the different jurisdictions is either omitted entirely, or is quite marginal.

These problems with international comparative research may be overcome, to some degree (cf. Nelken, 1994 and 2002). First, it is important not to leave the descriptions of the separate countries only to researchers from the countries concerned. In such cases it may be difficult to retain a common focus. As a result, an actual comparison between the countries will often be lacking, or it will only be minimal. For effective comparison the individual studies in the different jurisdictions must have a common focus right from the start. For instance, some elements in a certain country may be of interest only because of the contrast with other countries. If a common comparative perspective is lacking, such elements may remain unnoticed. Secondly, it is important that these studies are not based only on information collected from a distance. Researchers should visit the countries in person. They should conduct the interviews themselves and in some cases also the observations. Thirdly, for both practical and methodological reasons, international comparative studies should be limited to a small number of countries (Nelken, 2002). With a large number of countries in the sample, context-specific elements will lose their meaning and comparisons will only be possible at a fairly superficial level. The design of this comparative study rests on these three arguments.

Selection of the countries

This comparative study focuses on five different countries, selected on the basis of four criteria. First, each country should have a minimum level of plural policing. Secondly, the study will yield more information and insights if it deals with countries that have significant differences in plural policing. However, at the start we had no detailed information about plural policing in most countries. For this reason it was not possible to make a well-reasoned selection of countries on the basis of this argument. General considerations had to suffice. We therefore decided to select one non-European country, at least one country with a strong Anglo-Saxon orientation, and a country with a more continental European tradition, where neo-liberal ideology and notions of rolling back the state, or the need for a clear-cut distinction between 'steering' by the state and 'rowing' by other actors (Osborne & Gaebler, 1992) have generally had much less impact on government policy during the past two decades.
Thirdly, and rather in contradiction to the previous criterion, the situation in these countries should not differ too greatly with respect to plural policing. In this study we are interested in both public and private providers of policing, outside the regular police forces. For this reason, for instance, the U.S.A. is not included. In American cities the private security sector is so strong that as a rule there is no room for public wardens, guards and enforcement officers in addition to the public police (Manning, 2006). Considerable differences in social, political and economic context may also make comparison between jurisdictions difficult or even almost senseless. For this reason, countries like South Africa and Brazil have not been considered, even though both have a large private security industry that also works in the public or semipublic space.
Finally, practical considerations like travel time were also relevant. We decided to select only countries where we had the skills to interview and read documents in the native language so that we would not need to translate documents and use the services of interpreters.

In accordance with these criteria, five countries were included in this study: the Netherlands, England & Wales, Austria, Belgium and Canada. Austria was chosen as an example of a continental European country where the state has still retained much of its strong, traditional position. England & Wales was included as an example of an Anglo-Saxon country where neo-liberalism has had more impact than in most other European countries. Canada was selected as the non-European country. In Canada our study was limited to one province (Ontario), given the federal structure and significant differences in police structure between the provinces. At the start of our study we had some information showing that Ontario might be an interesting case, mainly because of the strong private component in plural policing. The Netherlands and Belgium were chosen as examples of different combinations of neo-liberal and continental elements. This sample of five different countries entitles us to assume that we can provide a varied analysis of international differences and developments in plural policing.

Methods of research

Each of the national studies consisted of a number of phases, with a different research method used in each phase. Moreover, a snowball method was used: each step delivered new information, new indications for sources of information, and names of persons who could be approached. Each step also produced new questions, the answers to which required new information. The following four phases can be distinguished.

a. Collecting relevant documents
First we started to collect and analyse relevant documents and publications about plural policing in the various countries. We used the internet and documentation systems, and consulted researchers in other countries, using our international professional relations. The availability of documents proved to differ markedly. In Austria, for instance, there is an almost complete lack of empirical research on plural policing and private security, in contrast to England & Wales or Canada. For this reason in Austria we had to rely mainly on non-scientific sources (such as internet documents), which means that the validity of this information is not always evident. In addition, in Austria and Belgium we did some research (mainly by interviews) at the local level, to get a more precise view of the practices of plural policing.

b. Additional information by e-mail
The analysis of the documents provided the first provisional answers to the questions that interest us. In addition, we found names and addresses of persons who might give us new information. We e-mailed these people, requesting additional information and other documents.

c. Interviews
After a preliminary analysis of the information thus gathered, six or seven key persons were interviewed in each country (with the exception of the Netherlands).[2] Because we already had a great deal of information available at that moment, we were able to ask these persons more specific questions.

2 Because the authors of this book are from the Netherlands it was not necessary to conduct interviews with key persons in this country. In the Netherlands we already had at our disposal a lot of information on plural policing, which had to be collected by means of interviews in the other four countries.

In total, 25 persons were interviewed. In most cases these were individual face-to-face interviews at the respondent's workplace. Only in England & Wales there was one group interview, with three persons working in the same organization.
These key persons were selected because they were experts on (some elements) of plural policing in their country and held a central position in their field. The key persons differ as to their position, field of activity, background, and expertise, and as a result in their perspective on plural policing. The key persons included were representatives of (national) ministries, social scientists working in this field of study, representatives of the police, local governments, and private security companies, as well as managers of non-police organizations providing policing services (see the Appendix for a list of the persons interviewed). Thanks to the combination of interviews with key persons with different expertise and social positions, and the analysis of documents and scientific literature, it was possible to produce a broad, detailed and very varied analysis of plural policing in each of the countries concerned.
The authors themselves conducted both individual interviews and the group interview. Each country was visited by one or two of the authors for a period of four to five days. During interviews we used a list of topics that we discussed with the key person. Although some general issues were discussed with all key persons, many of the specific topics differed not only from country to country, but also from person to person, depending on his or her special expertise and position.

d. Country reports

The information gathered was written up in country reports. These five reports had a more or less similar structure, based on the research questions mentioned above. The country reports were not published, but were used as the basis of the following chapters.

1.4 The structure of the book

The following chapters report the main findings and conclusions of this study. Chapters 2 to 6 present the analysis of plural policing in the Netherlands, England & Wales, Austria, Belgium, and Canada (Ontario), respectively. Each chapter has a more or less similar structure. Some general information is presented first about the country and the police system. Next, the main part of each chapter deals with the public providers of non-police policing services, followed by a description of the private guards and security officers working in the public space. Each chapter then goes on to deal with the cooperation with the public police, followed by a description of the rules and facilities for protecting citizens. Each country chapter concludes with a brief summary of the distinct patterns of

plural policing in the country concerned, and of the main issues in the public or political debate regarding this field.
The final chapter (7) deals with the main similarities and differences in plural policing between these jurisdictions. A typology is presented of the different forms of non-police providers of policing in the public space. Finally, four models are analysed that may be helpful to structure thinking and future public debate about plural policing.

2 The Netherlands

This chapter deals with plural policing in the Netherlands and especially the position of new wardens and enforcement officers in the public and semipublic space. The Netherlands (16.7 million inhabitants) is a Western European unitary state, with government and administrative institutions at three levels (central state, provincial and municipal). To understand plural policing in the Netherlands, one has to consider the position of the municipalities, which is especially important. In 2013 there were 408 municipalities in the Netherlands, differing greatly in size, from 790,000 (Amsterdam) to less than 2,000 (this despite a general increase of scale in the past few decades). Just as at the national level, local municipal council elections are held every four years. The mayor, however, who is the head of the local government, is not an elected official, but is appointed. One of the mayor's formal powers is that he/she has the 'authority' over the police in the territory of his/her municipality. The relative autonomy and formal powers of the municipalities relative to the central state and the province differ between the various policy domains.

Since the Second World War the Netherlands has seen drastic changes in social, political, cultural and economic respects. Originally, the Netherlands' economy was mainly based on agriculture; after the 1940s it accelerated a shift towards a highly industrialized nation. Nowadays the economy is to a great degree service-oriented, with a strong international focus. From the late 1960s, the densely populated country (the Western part is especially urbanized) shifted significantly from a strictly religiously pillarized, culturally conservative country to a more secular and permissive nation. Since the start of the 21st century, however, the country has once again been moving in very highly different political and cultural direction. Right wing and conservative views, albeit of a more late-modern style, have steadily been gaining ground. New right wing populist movements have scored significant electoral victories since 2001, a trend that has had a major impact on the political agenda and the presentation of politics in the mass media. Public concerns with safety, coupled with anti-immigrant sentiment, have contributed to and are reflected in this change, which is having major consequences for the social and political climate, notably with regard to policing and security in the Netherlands. The prevailing atmosphere has become more punitive, often with strong support for tough measures against crime and disorder (Downes & Van Swaaningen, 2007; Pakes, 2005 and 2006).

This chapter is structured similarly to the other national chapters. First, it deals briefly with the police system in the Netherlands. Although the country has had a new police system since January 2013, we also deal with the police structure as it existed previously, since the early 1990s. This regionalized police system in fact formed the main backdrop to and context for the pluralization of policing in the past two decades (2.1). We then go on to deal with the most important public (2.2) and private (2.3) non-police wardens and enforcement officers in the public and semipublic space. The relationships between these non-police providers of policing and the regular police are then analysed briefly (2.4), followed by a section on the protection of citizens against the abuse of formal powers by these new non-police wardens and enforcement officers (2.5). Finally, some more recent policy and other developments in this area are mentioned (2.6).

2.1 Police system

Until 1993 the Netherlands had a dual police system. Municipalities with more than 25,000 inhabitants had their own municipal police force. In addition there was the Royal Police force, which worked for the other areas of the country (such as smaller municipalities and rural areas) and carried out some tasks at national level.

The Police Act of 1993 replaced this dual police system by a regionalized system, consisting of 25 regional police forces and one national force. The central principle of this regionalized police system was 'decentralized, unless…'. According to this principle, at least during the first few years, significant elements both of the organization of the police forces and of the power to make decisions over the police were located at local and regional levels (Terpstra, 2004).

This Netherlands' regionalized police system was fairly complex, in both organizational and governmental terms. The 25 regional police forces were (more or less) independent. In principle they were seen as responsible for all relevant police tasks (the enforcement of public order, enforcement of the legal order (criminal investigation) and social services to citizens) in their territory. The regional forces differed greatly in size. Originally the national police force (KLPD) was intended to be additional to the regional forces, offering support to their work.

The post-1993 police system has a quite unique form of governance and accountability. Legally there are two forms of police governance: the *authority* over the police and the *administration* of the police. Each form of governance relates to different issues, with formal powers residing with different actors (Elzinga, 2007; Ministry of the Interior and Kingdom Relations, 2004).

The *authority* over the police involves the power to take decisions about actual police work, which involves decisions about police priorities, the use of police powers and the exercise of police work in a more general sense. In the regionalized system the authority over the police is a formal power vested in officials at local and regional levels. The Police Act distinguishes two forms of authority over the police. In relation to the enforcement of public order (including service tasks), the authority over the police lies with the mayor. The public prosecutor has authority over the police in regard to the enforcement of criminal law. Because the enforcement of public order and of criminal law are closely related, there is a need for regular consultation between the actors responsible for these two forms of authority. This is organized in what is called a 'local triangle', involving the mayor, the public prosecutor, and the local police chief.

The *administration* of the police involved the power to make decisions about the force's organization and resources (like human resources, financial budgets, material equipment, ICT systems and computerization). In the Netherlands' regionalized police structure the 'force administrator', who was usually the mayor of the largest municipality in the region, had this formal power. There was also a need for consultation at the regional level. In the regional triangle the force administrator frequently met with the (regional) principal public prosecutor and the regional police chief to consult on matters relating to the administration of the force.

In addition to the authority over and administration of the police, a third concept was distinguished, which is the *policy* of the police. At the regional level there was a Regional Board, consisting of the principal public prosecutor, the regional police chief and the mayors of all municipalities in the region. This Board had the task of establishing the policy of the regional police force.

All the officials just mentioned were appointed, not elected, which means that democratic accountability and control of the police in the Netherlands was quite an important issue. At the local and regional level this accountability was conferred on the democratically elected municipal councils. In practice, however, these local councils played only a minor role and had little influence in regard to police matters. This is the main reason why the regionalized police system in the Netherlands is often said to have a democratic deficit (Huberts et al., 2004; Van der Torre-Eilert, Bergsma & Van Duin, 2010).

Despite the original principle of 'decentralized, unless…', a creeping centralization of the police began quite soon after the introduction of the regionalized police system. Little by little, the national administration gained more influence on fixing the management and policy priorities of the police. The national police force (KLPD) gradually became an organization with an independent task, rather than having mainly a supplementary function for the regional forces. As a result of these centralizing forces since the late 1990s, notes of warning have increasingly been voiced against the growing distance between the Netherlands' police and the local governments and communities (Terpstra, 2004; Terpstra, 2013).

Since about 2005 the Netherlands' regionalized police system has been coming under increasing criticism. Several earlier proposals for reform to create a more centralized, national police force were unsuccessful for lack of support. However, in 2010 and 2011 the balance between proponents and opponents of the regionalized police system changed dramatically. In a remarkably short period of time political decisions were taken for a new reform of the Netherlands' police (Terpstra, 2013). From the beginning of 2013 the Netherlands has had a new, centralized national police force (Fijnaut, 2012).

This reform has had no consequences for the authority over the police, at least not formally. That formal power remains at the local level. In the national system too, authority over the police will be divided at the local level between the mayor and the public prosecutor. However, the 2013 police reform drastically changed the organization and management of the Netherlands' police.

A national police chief directs the national police force. He or she is responsible for the organization and management of the police. The national police force has ten areas, with a territorial division that runs parallel to that used for the criminal justice agencies and courts. In contrast to the previous police system, these police areas are not independent and have no formal discretion. As a result of the centralization of the police and the loss of independence by regional units, positions such as the force administrator (a position usually held by the major of the largest municipality in the region) and the regional Police Board have disappeared.

In the national police force the lowest organizational level consists of 'basic teams', which are responsible for all regular police tasks in their area. In the near future each of these teams is expected to have between 60 and 200 FTE (full-time equivalents). This would imply that the lowest level of the new national police will operate on a much greater scale than most of the basic teams of the previous regionalized police forces.

In the public debate about the establishment of a national police in the Netherlands a lot of attention was paid to the consequences it might have for the local position of the police, in both social and governmental terms. One question raised was whether the reform would mean the police would be operating at a greater distance from local communities. Some critics feared that locating the management and administration of the police at national level might have adverse consequences for the mayors' capacity to exercise their authority over the local police (Hennekens, 2011; Koopman, 2012; Terpstra & Gunther Moor, 2012).

2.2 Wardens and special investigative officers

Backgrounds

In the late 1980s the first new wardens or surveillance officers were introduced in the Netherlands. In line with the government policy of those days with regard to the administrative prevention of petty crime, it was deemed necessary to strengthen surveillance in the public space. In 1989 the first so-called City Guards (*Stadswachten*) went into operation. These schemes were not only based on considerations of public safety, but were also measures aimed at additional, usually temporary job creation for the long-term unemployed (Hauber et al., 1994). In the 1990s these state subsidized additional jobs were included in more general, more extensive schemes for the long-term unemployed. Many of these additional employment schemes have been closed down since 2004-2006. Since then, the people who worked as wardens or surveillance officers have been employed by the new, much larger municipal departments of City Surveillance or Local Enforcement (the departments are known locally by different names) (Van Steden, 2012).

In a more or less parallel development, local governments have been able to appoint so-called Special Investigative Officers (here we use the abbreviation SIOs: in Dutch *Buitengewoon Opsporingsambtenaren, BOAs*) since 1994.[1] These enforcement officers have the power to use certain sanctions (Fijnaut, 2012: 136-144).

From the late 1980s on, private security officers have also been gaining ground in the semipublic space in the Netherlands. As a rule, these officers were contracted by private enterprise, although the schemes were often organized as public-private partnerships. Initially these private security officers were mainly deployed in large industrial estates and business parks; later they were also to be found in shopping centres, railway stations and places of entertainment. Since the early 21st century, local governments in the Netherlands have also begun to contract employees of private security firms as wardens or Special Investigative Officers working in the public space.

In 1993 the Netherlands' police forces introduced police surveillance officers (*'politiesurveillant'*), also called police assistants (*'assistant politiemedewerkers'*). Compared to other police officers, police surveillance officers generally have a lower educational qualification, fewer powers of investigation, and generally do not carry firearms (although they often have a baton and pepper spray).[2]

The introduction of police surveillance officers should be seen as a reaction to the then recent rise of (municipal) City Guards. The police forces were hoping that the establishment of police surveillance officers would allow them to offer their own alternative to non-police city guards in the public space. The introduction of police surveillance officers was a strategy for the police forces to recover lost ground. At that time the Netherlands' Ministers of Justice and of the Interior argued that the introduction of police surveillance officers was necessary, given

1 The introduction of these officers was based on a ministerial decree on Special Investigative Officers of 1994 (http://wetten.overheid.nl/BWBR0007013/geldigheidsdatum_19-02-2013.).

2 Regeling aanstellingseisen politie 2002, http://wetten.overheid.nl/BWBR0014138/Bijlage5/geldigheidsdatum_09-09-2012, retrieved 13 March 2013.

the growing demand for surveillance in public space and the fragmentation of policing. This was said to make it hard to create effective cooperation between the police and the non-police (municipal) providers of surveillance. The Ministers had a favourable opinion of the introduction of (municipal) City Guards, but in their view the fact remained '*that it was necessary that the policy forces should intensify their own preventative and surveillance tasks.*'[3] The Ministers also expected that the institutionalization of police surveillance officers would result in a decreasing need for non-police surveillance in the public space.[4]

As a result of these initiatives and developments, the Netherlands today has a varied complex of public and private surveillance and enforcement personnel in the public and semipublic space. A variety of circumstances and changes have contributed to this (Terpstra, 2010: 147-158). In the early 1990s many citizens in the Netherlands began to attach a lot of weight to issues of public security. Feelings of insecurity, a supposed 'enforcement deficit' and the call for more uniformed officers on the streets ('*More Blue on the Streets!*' was and still is a popular political slogan in the Netherlands) have become more prominent. Despite the large increase of police officer numbers in the Netherlands over the last two decades (Haagsma et al., 2012), the police are increasingly deemed to be unable or unwilling to meet all the demands and needs placed on them. As a result there is an increasing tendency to let the police concentrate on its core (business) tasks (Terpstra, Gunther Moor & Van Stokkom, 2010).

At the same time it is becoming more important for politicians and governments to respond visibly to signs of feelings of insecurity and to the public's call for more surveillance and the enforcement of law and order. To a significant degree this responsibility often ends up in the hands of local governments. In the Netherlands the local government is viewed as the primary actor in local security policy. Here local governments are not only seen as responsible for creating the local security policy, they also act as the coordinator of the local security multi-agency networks (Terpstra, 2008). Since 2009 local governments in the Netherlands have gained more means to perform this central role in local security policy, thanks to the introduction of new legal instruments like administrative fines and the administrative penal order ('*bestuurlijke strafbeschikking*'). Both instruments give local governments more power to apply sanctions to citizens in the enforcement of law and order in the public space.[5]

Since the 1990s there has also been a process of responsibilization (Garland, 2001): citizens and companies are increasingly expected to take their own responsibilities for security. One of the strategies they use to realize this responsibility is

3 Second Chamber of the Netherlands' parliament, 1991-1992, Beleidsvoornemens politie 1992, p. 3, http://resourcessgd.kb.nl/SGD/19911992/PDF/SGD_19911992_0005184.pdf, retrieved 6 March 2004.

4 Ibid., p. 5.

5 See below in this chapter for more information on these powers of local government.

by contracting private security providers, not only for private domains, but also for semipublic and public spaces.
The increasing deployment of public and private guards, surveillance and enforcement officers is also a consequence of major changes in the urban space and economy. Security and security images have become more important to attract consumers, guests and tourists to large shopping centres, recreational areas, events, and tourist locations. The need for specialized (public and private) wardens, guards, and enforcement officers has also become more acute because many of the professional groups that used to have informal and secondary functions of social control have largely disappeared for reasons of economy and efficiency (Jones & Newburn, 2002).

Numbers

It is difficult to get an accurate view of the numbers of wardens and enforcement officers working in the public space in the Netherlands. The terminology used for these patrol, surveillance and enforcement professionals tends to differ between municipalities. Different groups of officers may be working in different cities in the Municipal Department for City Surveillance (as it may be called). In some cases, for instance, parking wardens and municipal 'environment protection officers' may also be included.
In 2010 the number of wardens and enforcement officers working in the public space was estimated at 4,200 FTE (Ministerie van Veiligheid en Justitie, 2010). This estimate, although frequently cited, is probably fairly unreliable. Another source of information states that in January 2013 there were 3561 Special Investigative Officers (SIOs) working in the public space in the Netherlands.[6]
The numbers of municipal wardens and SIOs working in the public space varies with the size of the municipality: the urban areas and the large municipalities commonly have more wardens and SIOs. However, even the large municipalities may differ greatly in the numbers of these officers, which may range from a few dozen up to 600 FTE (KplusV, 2010).

Powers and tasks

In the Netherlands it is usual to make a distinction between wardens and enforcement officers (Van Steden, 2012). Wardens usually have no special investigative or coercive powers. They have no more powers than 'ordinary citizens'. Their primary tasks consist of patrol, surveillance and guardianship in the public

6 This seems to suggest that there are only about 700 municipal wardens in the Netherlands. However, the study by the Ministry (2010) mentioned above shows that the numbers of municipal wardens almost equal the number of special enforcement officers. This implies that the reliability of all or some of these data is questionable.

space. Examples of these municipal wardens are City Guards ('Stadswachten') or City Surveillance Workers ('medewerkers Stadstoezicht') as they are called in some cities.

On the other hand, enforcement officers have special powers based on public law, which gives them the means to enforce certain rules. An example of these enforcement officers is the Special Investigative Officers (SIOs) (boa's) mentioned above. Usually both wardens and SIOs are paid municipal officials.[7]

In 1994 the Decree on Special Investigative Officers laid down rules for the position and powers of these officers, the requirements they should meet and the supervision of their work. These SIOs dispose of some legal policing powers and may (under certain conditions) use a limited amount of coercion.[8] As a rule SIOs have a limited investigative power, related to their position and job description. These investigative powers are conferred on an officer only if there is a direct need for such powers and for coercive means. The SIOs' licence will only be granted if the officer meets certain requirements for expertise (knowledge and skills) and standards of reliability for the implementation of the investigative powers.[9]

In 2011 the formal rules for the working domains, tasks, powers and equipment of the SIOs were elaborated in the form of a Ministerial Letter. A distinction is made between six working domains. One of these domains (the most relevant one in this context) is the public space (also known as Domain 1). SIOs working in this domain are mainly deployed for the 'fight against nuisance, social disorder and other circumstances that may have a negative impact on the quality of life.' According to this Ministerial Letter, Special Investigative Officers are only allowed to work in one domain and at the very most in two different municipalities.[10]

The SIOs have the legal authority to stop citizens and ask them for information, such as an identity card. Moreover, a SIO has the power to serve a summons on someone, to impose an administrative fine, and/or to impose an administrative penal order ('bestuurlijke strafbeschikking'), which may be the basis for a fine.

The (municipal) SIO working in the public space may have at his/her disposal handcuffs, baton, and pepper spray. The Ministry of Security & Justice may decide to place these means of coercion at the SIOs' disposal subject to the conditions that the officer's employer has demonstrated that these are necessary and

7 See below in this chapter for the exception of private security workers contracted by local governments.

8 The legal basis of these investigative powers is derived from art. 142 of the Criminal Code.

9 The Decree on Special Investigative Officers 1994, especially arts. 16 and 17 (*'Besluit Buitengeoon Opsporingsambtenaar 1994'*), retrieved at: http://wetten.overheid.nl/BWBR0007013/geldigheidsdatum_21-02-2013.

10 *'Circulaire Buitengewoon Opsporingambtenaar 2011'* (page 10), retrieved at: www.rijksoverheid.nl/documenten-en-publicaties/circulaires/2011/01/10/circulaire-boa.html.

that the officer meets the standards of capability and reliability. These standards are laid down in a special, formal arrangement.[11]

The Decree on Special Investigative Officers makes a distinction between supervision and direct supervision of the SIOs' work. The Public Prosecution Agency is responsible for the first form of supervision, which is concerned with the question of the extent to which the SIOs meet the standards of the Decree. As far as we know, no empirical research is available on how this supervision operates in practice. The second direct form of supervision is the responsibility of the police force. This is often also called operational steering by the police over the SIOs. It has to do with issues like 'the daily implementation, daily priorities, the provision of mutual support, the delivery of information, and cooperation' between the police and the SIOs.[12]

In practice, the municipal SIO's working in the public space have three main objectives: the enforcement of parking regulations (the issue of parking tickets, checking machines, and parking licences), patrolling in the public space and the enforcement of applicable rules, and regulation of specific problems such as nuisance, litter, dog dirt, and the probably typically Netherlands' urban problem of wrecked bicycles. Other issues that the SIOs focus on are the problematic behaviour of visitors in night-time areas and of groups of male youngsters hanging around on some street corners (Van Steden, 2012).

The uniforms of the SIOs (and also of the municipal wardens) differ between the municipalities. In practice they often resemble the police uniform. The only common element of their uniforms is that the SIOs are obliged to wear an SIO badge visibly during their work shifts.

Administrative fines and administrative penal orders

After many years of political debate and preparations, the Act on Administrative Fine for Disorder in Public Space ('Wet bestuurlijke boete overlast openbare ruimte') came into force in the Netherlands in January 2009. This law was intended to be an effective answer to the frequently noted enforcement deficit in regard to what was originally called 'petty annoyances in public space.' This law was to give the local governments more powers and means to fulfil their responsibilities in local security policy (Terpstra & Havinga, 2005). With the Act on Administrative Fine for Disorder in Public Space, municipal governments have

11 'Regeling Toetsing Geweldsbeheersing', retrieved at: http://wetten.overheid.nl/BWBR0021973/geldigheidsdatum_19-02-2013.

12 The Decree on Special Investigative Officers 1994 (*'Besluit Buitengeoon Opsporingsambtenaar 1994'*), retrieved at: http://wetten.overheid.nl/BWBR0007013/geldigheidsdatum_21-02-2013; Letter of the Minister of Security & Justice to the Chairman of the Second Chamber of the Netherlands' Parliament (*'Street Surveillance and Enforcement in Public Space'*), 24 March 2011, p. 4.

the administrative legal power to take action against prevalent forms of disorderly conduct in public space: municipal authorities can fine offenders.

Local governments are not obliged to use this system of administrative fines for the management of disorder. However, if a local government decides to use the system, it is fully responsible for its organization and implementation. In that case, however, there will still also be room for criminal law responses. In any case the police may still decide to take action on disorderly behaviour by fining a citizen, for instance if a situation escalates or if an offender is caught in the act. The implementation of these administrative fines for disorder in public space lies in the hands of the municipal SIOs. They do not impose the administrative fine themselves. Their role is only to announce the fine. The formal decision to impose the fine is taken later on by the local government or the mayor (Flight, Hartmann & Nauta, 2012: 10-13).[13]

Also since January 2009 the Netherlands has had the option of an administrative penal order ('bestuurlijke strafbeschikking') against disorderly behaviour. This also provides local governments with a means to take action against social disorder and nuisance without being dependent on the police. This administrative penal order system is also meant to make criminal law procedures more efficient and lessen the workload of the public prosecution agencies and the courts.

Like the administrative fines, these penal orders can be used to take action against prevalent forms of disorderly behaviour in the public space, like dog dirt, nuisance by groups of youngsters, or household refuse put out on the streets at the wrong time or in the wrong way. Unlike the system of administrative fines, the administrative penal order system is an integral part of criminal law procedures. However, in the first instance the procedure does not involve the court. The case can be taken to court only if a citizen objects to the local government.

Municipal governments are free to decide to use this system of penal orders. If they do, they have to inform the public prosecution agency in their region, in which case this agency will have to be restrictive in dismissing charges for administrative penal orders from this municipal government.

Municipal SIOs have formal power to give a citizen who has been involved in certain forms of disorderly behaviour notice of a penal order. The Central Collecting Agency of the Ministry of Security & Justice ('CJIB') is responsible for the rest of the procedure. The citizen pays the fines to this agency (Crijns, 2010; Flight, Hartmann & Nauta, 2012).

In sharp contrast to the initial high expectations and the promises that were made before the Netherlands' parliament finally decided on the Act on Administrative Fine for Disorder in Public Space, in 2012 not even one municipal government is using the system. About two-thirds of local governments decided to use the alternative system of administrative penal orders against disorderly behav-

13 Municipal Act (*'Gemeentewet'*) , art. 154b.

iour. For comparable reasons, it was already being suggested only one year after its introduction that the administrative fine system would soon be extinct (Crijns, 2010).

The study by Flight, Hartmann and Nauta (2012: 31-33) suggests several factors that may have contributed to this. First, municipal governments need fewer resources to implement the administrative penal order system than the system of administrative fines. The Central Collecting Agency of the Ministry of Security & Justice takes care of the administrative procedure. Municipal governments receive a fixed amount of money for each penal order made out by a municipal SIO. This amount of money is probably greater than what the municipal government would receive with an administrative fine for disorder.

Another important argument for municipal governments is that the system of penal orders creates more transparency and equality of rights. Under this system all municipalities have the same procedures and rules. It involves moreover the same procedures and rules as are used in criminal law enforcement.

2.3 Private security guards and special investigative officers

The Netherlands' private security industry has been growing strongly for about the past three decades. In 1981 the industry employed an estimated 10,000 persons. By 2011 the number of people working in Netherlands' private security industry had risen to about 32,000. There was also an increase in relative numbers: from 72 private security officers for every 100,000 inhabitants in 1981 to 196 in 2011 (Berghuis & De Waard, 2012).

Given this steep growth of the Netherlands private security industry, there was a general political consensus in the 1990s that it should be more tightly regulated. With this aim in view, the Act on Private Security Companies and Investigation Agencies ('Wet op de Particuliere Beveiligingsorganisaties en Recherchebureaus') was introduced in 1997. This Act requires private security companies to have a licence, which can be provided under certain circumstances by the Ministry of Security & Justice. The police organization is responsible for supervising the private security companies and for screening their new recruits.

It is sometimes assumed that government regulation of private security in the Netherlands is among the best in Europe (Button, 2007). Only a small number of studies are available about this regulation in practice. Their findings do not endorse such a positive evaluation. On the contrary, time and again the conclusion is that the regulation of private security in the Netherlands has many shortcomings (Terpstra, 2011).

One of the factors that have contributed to the growth of private security in the Netherlands is that the industry is increasingly becoming involved in activities in the public space. Since 2004 municipal authorities have had increasing legal scope to contract private security officers for surveillance and enforcement tasks in the public space (Ministerie van Justitie, 2004).

In the Netherlands, private security officers who work as (city) guards in public space have no special powers. However, that is not the case for employees of private security companies, who are contracted by a municipal government as a Special Investigative Officer (SIO) (Terpstra, 2012a). Since 2005 municipal governments have been legally permitted to use employees of private security companies as SIOs in the public space. SIOs are usually employed by a government agency. According to the Ministerial Letter mentioned above (Ministerie van Veiligheid & Justitie, 2011), municipal governments can contract 'a private official' as an 'honorary municipal official' who may have special investigative powers in the public space.[14] At the same time this private 'honorary municipal official' is still an employee of the private security company, but is under the direct hierarchical command of the municipal organization.

These private SIOs, as they may be called, have fewer formal powers at their disposal than other ('public') SIOs. A private SIO only has the power to demand an identity card, to issue fines for certain parking offences and offences against certain local ordinances.

If municipal governments wish to contract private SIOs, they have to fulfil certain conditions. The municipal council and the local triangle (the body consisting of the mayor, the public prosecutor, and the local police chief) have to agree. The use of private SIOs must fit in with the local security policy plan. The police are responsible for the daily coordination of the activities of the private SIOs, who must be recognizable as municipal officials. They are not permitted to wear any visible element that might be an indication to the general public that they are employed by a private security company.

The private SIO may have handcuffs 'at most', whereas his public colleague may also have a baton and a pepper spray at his/her disposal. According to the Ministerial Letter mentioned above, private SIOs have no access to police records or criminal investigation systems. Finally, a private SIO is not permitted to perform any activities for the private security firm or for a private investigation company as long as he or she is working as an SIO.

In 2010 about fourteen per cent of the Netherlands' municipal governments had contracted private SIOs (KplusV, 2010). Municipal authorities decide to use private SIOs for both managerial reasons and for considerations of security policy. As a rule, such municipal governments are confronted with problems of public safety, for which they deem it necessary to have a greater surveillance and enforcement capacity. A lack of resources, other priorities, or the view that this is not 'real police work' often mean that the police are not able or willing to provide

14 See also: Letter of the Minister of Security & Justice to the Chairman of the Second Chamber of the Netherlands' Parliament (*'Street Surveillance and Enforcement in Public Space'*), 24 March 2011, pp. 5-6.

the policing activities demanded. As a result, local governments decide to create or extend their own policing schemes. By contracting employees of private security corporations as SIOs they are able to create a more flexible organization. As the need for policing may fluctuate, capacity can be adjusted accordingly (Terpstra, 2012a).

The tasks and activities of private SIOs in the public space include: preventive patrol, collecting information (for the police and others), resolving problems of social disorder and quality of life (if necessary by means of rule enforcement), and the provision of services to citizens (such as tourists) (Terpstra, 2012a). These tasks and activities do not differ significantly from those of 'public' SIOs who are directly employed by the municipal organization (cf. Van Steden & Bron, 2012). In some cases municipal authorities hire private SIOs for more specific activities, one such instance being the 'street coach'. These officers are asked to engage in close relations with groups of boys/young men hanging around in certain areas (Van Steden & Jones, 2008).

The use of private SIOs by municipal governments is not without its problems. For example, the managerial notion of flexibility is often hard to reconcile with the need for the SIOs to build up detailed expertise, with up-to-date information about the neighbourhood, certain groups of youngsters, and locations with concentrations of problems, while having to sustain relations with both partners (the police, youth workers or janitor) and citizen groups (Van Steden, 2012; Terpstra, 2012a).

In the Netherlands private security officers are also used as wardens or patrollers in private and semipublic spaces, like business parks, malls, and large-scale events (Van Steden, 2007). Patrol, surveillance, guardianship, and the provision of services are the main tasks of these private security officers. If the officers are working in privately owned areas and are contracted by the owners of the locations, then they are permitted on behalf of the owner to deny entrance to persons or ask them to leave the grounds (Schuilenburg, 2012).

In addition, in the Netherlands there are a (presumably limited) number of private security officers who work in the public space but who are contracted by private agencies. Apart from private security workers who work in or in the direct vicinity of business parks and entertainment areas, there are also examples of residential patrols (in some cases combined with home alarm monitoring services). These are mainly to be found in (very) high-income neighbourhoods and are contracted by (organizations of) affluent inhabitants (Terpstra, 2010a). These private security officers have surveillance tasks only, and are not involved in enforcement. As far as we know, no empirical research has been done on this form of private security in the public space.

2.4 Relations with the police

In practice the relationships between these guards, wardens and enforcement officers and the (regular) police are often contradictory. On the one hand, the growth and rising importance of these non-police policing professionals are closely related to the fact that since the late 1990s the Netherlands' police have been withdrawing slowly from the 'front line'. First the police withdrew slightly from the villages and rural areas, based on the argument that more police resources should be made available to the larger cities. Later on, the police forces were strongly influenced by the core (business) task discourse. The emphasis on this issue meant that less attention was paid to elementary policing tasks, such as public visibility, patrol, and the prevention or management of social disorder (Terpstra, 2002; Terpstra & Kouwenhoven, 2004; Crijns, 2010; Terpstra, Gunther Moor & Van Stokkom, 2010; Terpstra, 2012a; Flight, Hartmann & Nauta, 2012).

This gradual withdrawal of the police has continued, despite the introduction of police surveillance officers in the early 1990s. The original intention underlying the introduction of these police surveillance officers was that the police forces would be able to provide an adequate answer to the growing need for surveillance in the public space. For reasons that are not entirely clear, police surveillance officers have proved not to be an adequate alternative to the increasing number of non-police municipal wardens.

As a result, most of the municipal governments in the Netherlands feel that they are more or less forced to do something about the gaps created by the withdrawal of the police. The result is that local governments started their own schemes of policing in the public space, consisting of both municipal wardens and SIOs.

In the Netherlands it is currently not unusual to speak about 'the new municipal police', which is quite ironic if one realizes that the police reform of 1993 (which paved the way for the 2013 police reform) abolished the old municipal police forces. Now it seems that after about twenty years of scale enlargement and centralization of the Netherlands' police, the local governments are back where it all started, creating their own municipal policing. The difference of course is that the new municipal policing officers do not dispose of full police powers, they are not an integral part of the (regular) police force, and they generally enjoy considerably lower social status (and authority).

In the Netherlands the police still have the formal power to act against disorderly behaviour, even in situations where municipal SIOs can also sanction this behaviour by means of an administrative fine or a penal order. Nevertheless, the existence of these enforcement alternatives may have the unintended consequence that the police will withdraw even further from these elementary tasks in the public space (Crijns, 2010).

On the other hand, however, according to the Ministerial Letter (Ministerie van Veiligheid & Justitie, 2011) mentioned above, the police are responsible for the daily or 'operational' coordination of the 'public' and private municipal SIOs in the public space.[15] This is quite a remarkable arrangement. In the Netherlands the coordination and leading role in local security policy lies not with the police, but is an important task of the municipal government. Moreover it is the municipal authorities, not the police, who are responsible for the policy and implementation of these new municipal policing schemes. This coordinating and policy role of municipal government may be expected to become even stronger and to be put on a legal basis in the near future. Finally, it is the municipal government that is to a great degree responsible for budgeting these municipal policing schemes. Nevertheless, the national government decided in 2011 that the police should have the daily coordination of the municipal SIOs working in the public space.

Several recent studies have shown that this operational coordination by the police often does not work very well (to put it mildly). There is often a wide gap between the police and the municipal SIOs. The provision of information by the police is often very poor (with some exceptions, mainly attributable to the high motivation and commitment of individual community police officers). The police rarely give concrete instructions. If the SIOs provide information to the police or if they have accomplished a task for the police, as a rule there is no feedback from the police. One of the factors contributing to this poor relationship is probably that police officers often have a rather poor view of the wardens and SIOs and the work they do. In their view, it has a far lower status than 'real' police work (Van Steden & Bron, 2012; Van Steden, 2012; Terpstra, 2012a).

2.5 Protection of citizens' rights

Usually citizens who do not agree with decisions by SIOs or the treatment they receive can use their municipal government's general complaints procedures. Especially in small municipalities there seems to be a tendency to process citizens' complaints in a primarily informal way. Citizens also have the opportunity to send these complaints to the National ombudsman, an independent national institution to which citizens can send their complaint about any aspect of the actions of the Netherlands' State (Van Steden, 2012). As far as we know, no empirical studies have examined how these procedures work in practice.

Citizens who do not agree with an imposed administrative fine have the formal right to object and appeal against the decision.[16] Citizens also have the right to appeal to the subdistrict court and may even appeal to a higher court (Flight,

15 See also: Letter of the Minister of Security & Justice to the Chairman of the Second Chamber of the Netherlands' Parliament (*'Street Surveillance and Enforcement in Public Space'*), 24 March 2011, pp. 3-4.

16 The General Act Administrative Law (*'Algemene Wet Bestuursrecht'*) , art. 8:1 and 7:1.

Hartmann & Nauta, 2012: 12). Because there is no municipality in the Netherlands that uses the system of administrative fines for disorder, these complaint and appeal procedures are only paperwork.
If a citizen wants to object to an administrative penal order, he/she can protest the decision before the Public Prosecution Agency. Next, citizens can appeal against the decision before the subdistrict court and may even appeal to a higher court (Crijns, 2010). Once again, as far as we know, no empirical studies have attempted to answer the question of how often these procedures are used and how they work in practice.

2.6 Some future developments

Over the past few years there have been some new policy and other developments in plural policing in the Netherlands. Although these are still in an early stage, they may have important consequences for the future positions of municipal wardens and enforcement officers in this country. Three such developments are briefly as follows.
First, there are some indications that the Netherlands' government may want to extend the formal powers of the municipal SIOs working in the public space. In March 2012 the Minister of Security & Justice announced some pilot schemes that will also give these SIOs enforcement powers in regard to environmental protection. Depending on the outcomes of these schemes, it might mean that future municipal SIOs working in the public space will have a broader policing role and more formal powers.[17] In addition, since 2012 the government has also started five pilot schemes with so-called Shop SIOs (*'winkelboa's'*). This new category of SIO should contribute to combating shoplifting. For the past few years it seems that the regular police often do not devote a great deal of time and resources to this problem. In these schemes the task of the police is taken over to a significant degree by the municipal SIOs. The government wants shop owners who are victims of shoplifting to stop calling the police, but instead call the municipal SIOs. In that case the SIOs will go to the store, assist the owner with making up the crime report, hear witnesses, and look at the available evidence, such as example CCTV camera images. If necessary, the SIOs will also conduct a body search of the suspect and take him/her to the police station, where the police can take custody of the suspected person and pursue the subsequent steps in the criminal law procedure.[18]
Secondly, in the near future the government may be expected to seek to reduce local differences in the ways the municipal SIO's operate in the public space. For

17 Letter of the Minister of Security & Justice to the Chairman of the Second Chamber (*'Progress professionalization surveillance and enforcement in the public space'*) , 5 March 2012, p. 2.

18 Idem. See also: Flight, Hartmann and Nauta (2012).

example, the government wants municipal SIOs throughout the country to wear the same uniform in future.[19] In 2011 the government also announced that the supervision of the municipal SIOs by the Public Prosecution Agency and the police should be more standardized.
Thirdly, although municipal governments have increasingly been contracting private security companies for surveillance and enforcement tasks in the public space since 2005, it is not self-evident that the number of private SIOs will steadily increase. It looks as if the government has recently become more reluctant to allow local authorities to contract private security companies for these tasks. In March 2011 the Minster of Security & Justice declared that in his view there is no room for a private municipal police (or even 'the appearance of such'). In his view, too, another form of quasi-market in local policing in the Netherlands should be terminated. Municipal authorities should no longer recruit or hire officers of the regular police force. Existing contracts between municipal authorities and police forces should, in his view, be terminated in a 'decent manner' (whatever that may mean).[20] At the time of writing it is not clear whether these developments are signs of more radical changes in the Netherlands government's policy with regard to the pluralization of policing at the local level.

19 Letter of the Minister of Security & Justice to the Chairman of the Second Chamber (*'Progress professionalization surveillance and enforcement in the public space'*) , 5 March 2012, p. 2.

20 Brief van minister van Veiligheid & Justitie aan Voorzitter van Tweede Kamer ('Straattoezicht en Handhaving in de openbare ruimte'), 24 maart 2011, pp. 6-7.

3 England & Wales

England & Wales (55 million inhabitants; Office for National Statistics, 2011) are part of the United Kingdom (together with Scotland and Northern Ireland). England & Wales are the constitutional successor of the former Kingdom of England, and have the same legal system: English Law.

The police in England and Wales consist of 43 territorial police forces (Mawby & Wright, 2008). In 2011 the police employed a total of 243,000 persons, over 140,000 of whom were sworn police officers. Over 80,000 employees comprise the civilian staff (Home Office, 2012).

Recent decades have witnessed an increase of policing by organizations other than the police. A complex division of labour has evolved in policing and security. The idea of a police monopoly as the guardian of public order (which arose with the advent of the professional police in England and Wales in the nineteenth century) has been abandoned. The police are increasingly viewed as just one of the organizations involved in surveillance and control within the public space. In this context, the current jargon speaks of the 'extended policing family', including security partnerships and networks, in which wardens and private security guards also play a role (Crawford, 2008: 147). What is remarkable, however, is that the police have managed, with the introduction of the Police Community Support Officers (PCSOs) in 2002, to retain surveillance work in the public space for the most part within their own organization.

The architect of the PCSOs was the London police chief Ian Blair. He was initially in favour of the idea that the police had to adjust to the evolving pluralistic security field. The police would have to abandon their monopoly claim on street surveillance and should focus on coordinating surveillance and enforcement agencies. In 2002 he modified his view, assuming that police officers were not sufficiently visible. Private security patrols and Warden schemes would lead to a 'Balkanization' of policing in London. He argued that the police should retain their role as dominant supplier of services. Because of the PCSOs the force could reconsolidate its sovereignty over community policing in London (Johnston, 2003: 196-198).

This chapter is structured as follows. Section 3.1 describes some relevant developments in national police policies. Section 3.2 deals with the way PCSOs function.

Section 3.3 then goes on to discuss some developments with regard to neighbourhood wardens. Section 3.4 describes the role of the private security guards in the public space. Subsequently, some of the findings are discussed regarding cooperation between surveillance officers and the police (3.5) and the protection of citizens (3.6). Some current issues that have elicited much debate in England and Wales are briefly discussed in section 3.7.

3.1 Police system and policy

Partnerships

From the beginning, New Labour policy (1997-2010) put a strong emphasis on the prevention and control of disorderly and anti-social behaviour. In this regard, Labour policymakers distanced themselves from the then dominant logic that the main police task consists of mere 'crime control' (Barker and Crawford, 2013). Partnerships and community safety emerged as guiding principles of local safety policies. The Crime and Disorder Act (1998) assigned responsibility for reducing crime and disorder to newly formed partnerships, Crime and Disorder Reduction Partnerships (CDRPs). The legal responsibility for fighting crime and anti-social behaviour was thus delegated to local bodies.

The philosophy of New Public Management (NPM) occupied a central place in the management of such partnerships. The Home Office took control of the partnerships by imposing quantifiable targets and promoting an 'audit culture'. In fact, the local partnerships in England were not given much room for autonomous decision-making. The partnerships were therefore not genuinely connected to what actually happened in the neighbourhoods. They operated in a 'technocratic niche', more or less isolated from the expectations of the local population (Hope, 2005; Hughes, 2004). After the coalition government came to power in 2010, the partnerships started to operate much more flexibly.[1]

During the long period of New Labour's reign, the police organization actually became increasingly centralized. The Police Reform Act (2002) and the Police and Justice Act (2006), for example, gave more power to central government and the Home Office (Mawby & Wright, 2008). The far-reaching influence of the audit and inspection bodies and the pay-for-performance system meant that policing was local in name only. It was the Home Office targets, not local interests, that mainly determined policy priorities (Loveday, 2013).

1 Interview with respondent 1 England & Wales.

Reassurance policing

After 2000 'reassurance policing' became a dominant policy theme. Policy makers were faced with paradoxical developments: while crime rates declined, subjective insecurity among the population increased; at the same time confidence in the police continued to decline. This phenomenon was known as the 'reassurance gap'. To overcome this problematic trend the police were to focus more on the prevention of negative public perceptions and regain public trust (Innes and Fielding, 2002). The police would have to act as a 'reassurance factor', increasing their visible presence on the streets. Citizens would feel reassured if they have the idea that 'everything is under control' and that disorderly behaviour is being addressed.

Between 2003 and 2005, Reassurance Policing was introduced in eight forces. After a successful evaluation, the programme was implemented nation-wide in the National Neighbourhood Policing Programme, which has led all forces to introduce 'safer neighbourhood teams', which are expected to focus their attention on those problems that residents indicate as most acute.

This new policy entailed a considerable increase in front-line staff. The Police Community Support Officers (PCSOs), who had made their entrance with the Police Reform Act of 2002, were the chosen vehicle. They were to maintain a visible presence on the streets, without the 'tyranny of the radio' and other reactive tasks that often hamper visibility (Barker & Crawford, 2013).

The influential London police chief Ian Blair was a leading advocate of the PCSOs. As mentioned, he turned against the increase of private security in the public space and the fragmentation of the surveillance functions, pleading for consolidation and strengthening of the surveillance function within the police (see Johnston, 2003).

The Police Reform Act (Section 41) also introduced the concept of an 'accredited employee'. Under the Community Safety Accreditation Scheme (CSAS), citizens (special constables), wardens and private security guards (such as security officers in shopping malls) could be granted modest police powers, including the issue of fines for minor infringements (Crawford et al., 2005). Accredited employees are also allowed to participate in the local crime and disorder partnerships. The granting of powers is the purview of the local Chief Officer of Police. One of the ideas behind this is that wardens and private security guards would behave more responsibly if, for example, they were commissioned by a housing corporation to do surveillance work.

PCCs and cuts

The coalition government of Prime Minister Cameron – which assumed power in 2010 – has explicitly turned against the centralizing tendency within the police. The police, they hold, should be controlled far more by the local administration and the local population. The police in England and Wales are currently undergoing a major reform. As from late 2012, the territorial police forces are no longer controlled by Police Authorities but by Police and Crime Commissioners (PCCs), a development arising from the Police Reform and Social Responsibility Act 2011. The PCCs are directly elected by the populace, which is supposed to ensure that the police can better anticipate the needs and priorities of local communities (Barker and Crawford, 2013).[2] The tasks of the PCCs include: determining the strategic direction of the police force, taking responsibility for the effectiveness and efficiency of policing within the corps, controlling expenses and management within the force, and looking after the interests of the populace (especially the vulnerable and victims) (Home Office, 2011). Police and Crime Panels are to be established to oversee the work of the PCCs. These panels must consist of at least one elected representative (alderman or elected mayor) from each municipality covered by the police force, and two independent members appointed by the panel.[3]

The coalition government believes that police numbers should be radically decreased and that resources should be deployed in 'smarter' ways. The influence of the formula 'bigger budget = more staff = better policing' should be broken. In the period 1999-2009, expenditure on the police increased by 88% (Loveday 2013). The coalition government announced a 25% cut in central government budgets between 2010 and 2014 (Barker & Crawford, 2013), which means that – according to the Inspectorate of Constabulary (HMIC) report *Policing in austerity. One year on* (2012) – more than 30,000 jobs would have disappeared by 2015, and thousands of jobs will also disappear from frontline work, including 1,700 PCSOs. The underlying idea is that officers who perform back-office tasks should have a higher profile in the frontline. At the same time, there are plans to deploy more special constables and other volunteers to do visible, street-level police work. The HMIC report *'Valuing the Police'. Policing in Austerity* (2010) stated the intention to increase the number of special constables in England & Wales from 15,500 in 2010 to 24,500 in 2015. According to this report, these police volunteers would be able to do police work in the public domain and thus contribute to 'reassurance'. At the same time the report suggests that the larger group of

2 In November 2012 only 16% of the population turned out for the election of the PCC for 41 forces (without greater London and London City): www.telegraph.co.uk/news/uknews/law-and-order/9685097/Theresa-May-defends-Police-Commissioner-elections-after-low-turnout.html, retrieved 03 January 2013.

3 Home Office website, www.homeoffice.gov.uk/police/police-crime-commissioners/public/accountability, retrieved 9 October 2012.

volunteer police officers could fill the gap that would be created by a reduction in the number of professional police officers in the front line.[4]

Finally, the coalition government expects a great deal from the further privatization of police functions. Within the Business Partnering for Police programme, the transfer of office functions to the private sector is high on the agenda (Loveday, 2013). Even before the coalition government came to power, the Lincolnshire Police had signed a £ 200 million contract with G4S to build and staff a police station. The security company is expected to perform custody services and other tasks. Half the civilian staff are to join the private company. The West Midlands and Surrey forces subsequently adopted even broader initiatives, involving a tender of £ 1.5 billion. Following the Lincolnshire experiment, the work of police staff is to be handed over to private companies. PSCOs may also be in line for similar private management. After the 'G4S fiasco' (the security company was unable to deliver the security staff for the Olympics in London in July 2012), these plans have once again come under debate (Barker & Crawford, 2013).

3.2 Police Community Support Officers

Police Community Support Officers (PCSOs) are surveillance officers who work for the vast majority of their time on the streets, dealing with petty crime and nuisance. They have less training and fewer powers than ordinary police officers and they count as 'civilians'. PCSOs work within the police organization and are managed by the police; they give the police the opportunity to enlarge their visible presence on the streets and thus increase public reassurance. Regular police officers would therefore have more time to perform tasks that are better suited to their higher level of education, skills and competence (Crawford et al., 2005: 7-13).

In England & Wales, 15,612 PCSOs were employed in September 2011 (Home Office, 2012). This is a slight decrease compared to previous years, which seems to be due to the cuts to the police service (Barker and Crawford, 2013).

Many types of PCSO are active, especially in London, on such duties as traffic, parks and schools. In 2007 the Metropolitan Police Service employed more than

4 Special constables have the full powers of police officers. According to one of the interviewees, a great deal of effort in the Home Office department responsible for the development of special constables is currently being devoted to attracting more volunteers (with expense allowances, training, etc.). He points out that in recent years the number of volunteers within the police has grown to about 20,000 (13% of the total number of police officers). See also: www.policeoracle.com/news/Local+and+Neighbourhood+Policing/2012/Jul/16/ACPO-Lead-Specials-Are-Not-Policing-On-The-Cheap_51167.html, retrieved 28 December 2012.

3,000 PCSOs (Davey, 2011). According to one respondent[5] this number has now dropped to 1,800 for a variety of reasons.

Tasks and powers

The fundamental task of PCSOs is to contribute to the policing of neighbourhoods through visible surveillance work. Important tasks are: reassuring the public, increasing public order and being accessible to citizens and partner organizations working at the local level. The powers necessary to carry out these tasks vary from neighbourhood to neighbourhood and from force to force (ACPO, 2007, Section 3). PCSOs are supposed to spend 80% of their time on visible surveillance. This target is mainly a response to the limited time (slightly more than 40%) that regular police officers can spend on the streets (Crawford et al., 2005: 55-58). PCSOs generally work in defined neighbourhoods. In addition, they often work in city centres and often are deployed at hot spots (Paskell, 2007: 354).

PCSOs are required to postpone the use of coercive measures during their work as long as possible, solving problems in an informal and consensual way. This is important for maintaining good relations between themselves and the public.[6]
The powers of PCSOs are laid down in the first paragraph of Schedule 4 of the Police Reform Act 2002. There are three categories of powers. First, there are a number of standard powers that every PCSO has, such as issuing a fine for cycling on a footpath, seizure of alcohol in the possession of minors, seizure of drugs, requesting personal data (for example in relation to nuisance or consuming alcohol in public), and a number of traffic-related powers (placing signs, ensuring that abandoned vehicles are removed, etc.).
Besides these general powers, there are powers that may be conferred by Chief Officers, such as issuing fines for nuisance, dog mess, truancy and graffiti, returning minor children (<16) to their homes, and returning truants to their school. This category also includes powers to stop and search people. The final category, which is also conferred by Chief Officers, is the imposition of fines for the violation of certain by-laws, such as enforcing the ban on selling alcohol to persons under the age of eighteen, possession of fireworks, giving false information to the police, public drunkenness, and giving a false alarm to the emergency services.

5 Source: interview with respondent 6 England & Wales.
6 It was not considered a good idea that PCSOs should work as traffic wardens, who issue a lot of fines and have thus acquired a poor image (Merritt, 2010: 742).

With regard to making arrests PCSOs have no more powers than ordinary citizens. This means that they may use 'proportionate and reasonable force' to protect themselves and others.[7]

The quality requirements for PCSOs can be found in the Police Reform Act 2002.[8] PCSO training takes between four and six weeks and should include components such as multi-ethnicity, ethics, social skills, first aid, self-defence, problem-solving approaches to crime and disorder, understanding powers and legislation on anti-social behaviour. In practice there appear to be problems with the training of PCSOs: there are great differences in quality between the training programmes offered (Johnston, 2007).

Section 9 of the *Guidance of Police Community Support Officers* (ACPO, 2007) states that PCSOs should have mobile phones and/or a notebook at their disposal, and equipment that is suitable for the health and safety risks expected in the performance of their work. Their kit could include bulletproof vests, pepper spray, batons and handcuffs.
The Police Reform Act 2002 states that PCSOs should wear recognizable clothing, which should be distinct from the clothing of regular police officers.[9] The Home Office wants PCSOs to have a similar appearance in the whole country.[10]

Implementation within Safer Neighbourhood Teams

Generally speaking, PCSOs work within Safer Neighbourhood Teams (SN teams). As noted earlier, these teams are based on the concepts and insights of reassurance policing. The teams consist of one sergeant, two police officers and three PCSOs. Safer neighbourhood teams focus on the specific security needs of their neighbourhood. They should involve their local community in establishing and negotiating priorities for action and in identifying and implementing solutions. Priority setting mainly involves quality of life issues, such as anti-social

7 Section 38 of the Police Reform Act 2002, which refers to Section 3 (1) of the Criminal Law Act 1967 in conjunction with relevant jurisprudence. In some force areas, chief constables have the option to grant their PCSOs a limited power of detention (detaining a person for a period until a police officer arrives).

8 Section 38 of the Police Reform Act 2002.

9 Section 43 of the Police Reform Act 2002.

10 The general pattern of this uniform is (ACPO, 2007, Section 9): *'peaked cap (for men) or bowler hat (for women), with plain dark blue band and enamel cap badge without royal crest but bearing the words "Community Support Officer" or "Police Community Support Officer", Black or Blue anoraks, or reflective yellow / part reflective yellow, part blue jacket with the designation "Community Support Officer" or "Police Community Support Officer" in white on blue background with separate police force crest/logo, White or Blue uniform shirt, Royal blue epaulettes and tie, Standard issue or dark blue uniform trousers.'*

behaviour, abandoned cars and graffiti.[11] The teams should adopt an intelligence-led, proactive, problem-solving approach to enable them to focus on and tackle specific local issues. The teams ensure a two-way flow of information with the community to build trust and cooperation, to help them deal more effectively with crime and anti-social behaviour (Home Office, 2004).
A recent report (Davey, 2011) shows that it is difficult for the SN teams to focus on surveillance. They are also tasked with other activities, such as emergency first-response and handling nuisance notifications, partly because other local departments fail in that regard. Like the emergency teams, in practice, SN teams should focus more on reducing crime. The SN teams therefore do not devote enough of their time to their core tasks of reassurance, citizen engagement, and problem solving, and they are less visible on the streets than was intended.

Evaluation studies

A national evaluation (Cooper et al., 2006) shows that PCSOs spend a relatively large amount of time on alcohol-related issues, petty crime and anti-social behaviour, and the disciplining of unruly youth. Residents have proved to be more willing to speak to these officers than to police officers. They are also satisfied with the PCSOs, especially when they are known in person. They believe the PCSOs have an impact on tackling youth nuisance. Many PCSOs are of the opinion that they are vulnerable to hazardous situations; a substantial minority have had to deal with physical violence. According to Cooper and colleagues (2006) the PCSOs are worried about their future career, most of them viewing their work as a stepping stone to the regular police. One potential disadvantage of this is staff turnover, resulting in a loss of familiar faces on the streets.
The research by Crawford and colleagues (2004) on PCSOs in West Yorkshire (Leeds and Bradford) shows that the public is pleased with them. The vast majority of the public identify an actual increase in the number of surveillance officers. They feel safer and are satisfied with the way PCSOs tackle problems.
Other research (Paskell, 2007: Foster & Jones, 2010) shows that PCSOs are able to make contact with residents. Residents prefer to have these officers in the neighbourhood, rather than the regular police. They view PCSO work as not so much about enforcement but about providing services. The relative lack of power and authority works precisely to their advantage. Although the PCSOs were initially seen as 'plastic police' or 'mobile scarecrows' (getting in the way of the regular police officers), they delivered an effective contribution to strengthening the local order. Many young people are afraid to be recognized and, according to Paskell, many are deterred from vandalism by PCSOs.

11 Website of the London Metropolitan Police: http://content.met.police.uk/Site/saferneighbourhoods, retrieved 27 September 2012.

A more recent study (Merritt, 2010) shows that the role of the PCSOs is slowly shifting towards law enforcement. PCSOs act not so much as surveillance officers who are expected to reassure the public, which was the intention at their introduction in 2002, but more as 'junior enforcers'. They are also viewed less as bridge builders and community workers. The PCSOs are heading into a role in which they can increase the 'productivity' of the police. This productivity lies in activities such as more frequent visiting of victims, initiating the investigation of petty crime, and a continued focus on intelligence gathering (Merritt, 2010). However, the role of bridge builder has still not been abandoned, the more so because it seems to be critical to the success of PCSOs (Merritt, 2010: 746).
Regular discussions take place about whether the powers of PCSOs should be extended to include, among other things, dealing with addicts and aggressive beggars, and the questioning of detainees. Many fear that this expansion will be at the expense of their ability to peacefully gain the consent of citizens (Merritt, 2010; Johnston, 2007).

Has the PCSO to a greater extent become an enforcer? One interviewee points out that the reassurance part of their work has been compromised. Tackling local problems and issues is also receiving less attention. This respondent does not believe that the powers of PCSOs will be expanded, however, and believes that the PCSOs will never be 'armed'.[12] Some respondents believe that there is no question of a shift to a more repressive approach by the PCSOs. One of the respondents considers that the whole concept of the PCSOs remains unchanged: it still comes down to tackling anti-social behaviour and functioning as 'eyes and ears' of the police.[13] Another respondent points to the problem that the PCSO function has become a kind of stepping-stone to moving up within the police organization. For that reason, according to this respondent, there is less continuity: PCSOs are less committed to a specific neighbourhood and do not view their work on the street as attractive.[14] Other respondents recognize this: in recent years PCSOs have enjoyed greater opportunities to become a police officer.

3.3 Neighbourhood wardens

Besides PCSOs, different types of wardens (neighbourhood wardens, street wardens, and street crime wardens) have been incorporated into the landscape of local security. These are surveillance officers in the public space who have no

12 Interview with respondent 6 England & Wales.
13 Interview with respondent 2 England & Wales.
14 Interview with respondent 5 England & Wales.

additional powers. They are usually employed by municipalities, but sometimes also by housing associations (Crawford & Lister, 2006).[15]

In 2000, the national government decided to fund the development of warden schemes, first with the Neighbourhood Warden Programme and in following years with other programmes. The objective was to improve the quality of life in the local environment (Crawford et al., 2005: 8).

Recent estimates of numbers of wardens are difficult to find, but probably a few thousand wardens are active. In 2004 there were approximately 3,500 wardens, but they seem to have fallen in number since the emergence of the PCSOs (Crawford, 2008: 158).

Wardens are an important part of the National Strategy for Neighbourhood Renewal (Social Exclusion Unit, 1999). Policy makers were inspired by various European projects, including the Dutch city wardens (*stadswachten*).

One of the reasons for introducing wardens was the continued centralization of housing management. The withdrawal of housing associations from the neighbourhoods was accompanied by growing nuisance and neglect of the housing stock (Scanlon, 2006).

Tasks and powers

The following tasks are important. First, the wardens should improve the quality of life by providing a uniformed presence in neighbourhoods. They should promote safety in the neighbourhoods, contribute to neighbourhood development and assist in improving the environment and housing management. An additional role is to reduce local crime and disorder (Neighbourhood Renewal Unit, 2002).

In their role as 'eyes and ears', wardens are intended to provide a direct link between the local residents and local agencies (in particular the local authorities, the police and housing associations). They are expected to listen to the worries and problems that occupy the people, and report them to the authorities concerned. They also have the task of bridge building in the local community, promoting local initiatives, and they have tasks in relation to the environment and vacant housing (Social Exclusion Unit, 1999; Crawford et al., 2005: 34).

The description of the tasks and duties of wardens is deliberately broad, since it gives them the latitude and flexibility needed to deal with many different problems. Wardens have no more powers than any other citizen. They are surveillance officers and can only address citizens and inform / warn them (Crawford et al., 2005: 43-44).

The (quality) requirements for wardens are determined locally; no national standards have been formulated. The wardens' equipment is also specified locally. For example, Bradford City Centre wardens have a mobile phone and a stab

15 By contrast traffic wardens are supervised by the police.

vest (Crawford et al., 2005: 100). Their uniforms too are local matters. An Internet search yields numerous hits for companies that sell warden uniforms and equipment.[16] Private security guards sometimes take on the role of warden (Johnston, 2003).

Evaluation studies

A national evaluation of warden projects was published in 2004, funded by the national programme. It showed that between 2001 and 2003 residents in the pilot areas experienced significantly less crime, with a decrease of about 25%. In the control neighbourhoods (without wardens), there was a slight increase (Neighbourhood Renewal Unit, 2004). Citizens were significantly more satisfied with their neighbourhood, and also saw improvements in environmental problems such as graffiti, litter and dog fouling. According to the report the most distinctive feature of the warden programme is that wardens are community based; their advantage lies in their accessibility to people, listening to problems and worries; they function as a link between residents and service providers.
Another report that evaluated Warden Schemes in the early stages reaches similar conclusions (Coward et al., 2004). Based on three case studies, the researchers conclude that Warden Schemes constitute an adequate response to a series of problems, ranging from anti-social behaviour, to decay and fear of crime. As wardens engage more closely with the community and support vulnerable groups, they succeed in winning the trust of the public, including teenagers. According to the authors, a more passive 'eyes and ears' role fits less well with the wardens, and since the emergence of the PCSOs this warden role has become more or less obsolete.[17]

The Warden Schemes of Leeds and Southampton were examined in separate studies (Crawford et al., 2005 and Scanlon, 2006, respectively). Forty-five wardens were appointed in Leeds (720,000 inhabitants) in 2003. According to Crawford (2006b) wardens help to improve social relations between residents and local agencies, especially in disadvantaged neighbourhoods. This conclusion is consistent with the findings of the other national reports cited above. This study also found that there is little clarity about the wardens' tasks. Wardens in Leeds are actually concerned with the improvement of the physical environment, and they act as a go-between between authorities and difficult-to-reach groups. They maintain their distance from the police so they can be trusted by such groups. Nevertheless, there are pressures to draw wardens into more security-oriented func-

16 See for example: www.kelticclothing.co.uk/jobroles/enforcementuniforms.html, retrieved at 27 September 2012.

17 However, respondent 2 England & Wales points out that in Westminster (London) the neighbourhood wardens focus less on the local community and act more as enforcement officers.

tions. For example, many local politicians are in favour of wardens obtaining accreditation, so that they can impose fines. This would transform their relationship with residents into a more antagonistic one and place them in conflict situations. According to Crawford (2006b: 973), the emergence of PCSOs in areas where wardens work has had two effects. First, where wardens performed no clearly defined tasks, there was an inclination to regard them as doing security work. In this context they were identified as poor alternatives to PCSOs, given their lack of powers. Secondly, if enough resources are available and a clear division of labour between wardens and PCSOs has been articulated, wardens could focus more on their community development tasks.
In Southampton (220,000 inhabitants) 35 wardens were appointed citywide in 2005. These wardens are employed in the municipal Housing Department. The study (Scanlon, 2006) showed that wardens themselves largely determine their daily tasks, which makes it very difficult to monitor their activities. By far the most time is spent on cleaning streets and parks. They report criminal behaviour directly or indirectly (through the Housing Department) to the police, but do not consider reducing nuisance and petty crime as their primary tasks. The population is positive about their work.

These evaluations show that wardens do operate independently of the police. They are usually managed by the municipal Housing Department. A major problem for the continuity of Warden Schemes is funding. In the initial phase, between 2000 and 2005, about 250 Schemes were funded by national government (initially within the New Deal for Communities programme). Those funds were then cut and municipalities now have to provide their own funding.

Most respondents acknowledge that the number of wardens fell after the rise of the PCSOs, to the regret of some. One respondent had a strong opinion on this subject:

> 'The wardens here in Portsmouth have ensured that people in neighbourhoods want to think along. They have direct lines with various local service organizations and through that network they can refer people quickly and provide appropriate assistance. They are also very present in the neighbourhood, much more than the police could ever do. They have played a major role in tackling anti-social behaviour. And because of their engagement they were accepted by the people. They also came to know much about local issues. They became walking encyclopaedias of what happens in the communities. This is incredibly valuable.'[18]

18 Interview with respondent 5 England & Wales.

3.4 Private policing

Alongside the introduction of PCSOs and wardens, there has also been an increase in the number of private security guards operating in public and semipublic space (Jones & Newburn, 2006b; Crawford et al., 2005: 13). This growth can be attributed to the following factors. First, private security guards are increasingly deployed in areas of mass private property (shopping centres, leisure arenas, sports stadiums, etc.) and residential enclaves (Crawford & Lister, 2006; Jones & Newburn, 2006b: 44). Private security guards have also been employed in Business Improvement Districts (BID's) (Cook, 2010). In addition, the expansion of the entertainment sector (pubs, clubs, etc.) has contributed to the growth of private security guards in semipublic space (Crawford, 2008: 168-169).

It is striking that security firms have hitherto made hardly any use of Community Safety Accreditation Schemes (see section 3.2.2), which provide private security guards with greater powers and might possibly raise their 'public status'; the costs perhaps scare off many companies. Moreover, not all chief constables are willing to confer greater powers on security guards because they are fundamentally opposed to their deployment in the public space. These schemes are mainly used by wardens. By late 2010 only 2,200 people had been accredited, spread across 26 participating forces (Crawford and Lister, 2003; Barker and Crawford, 2013).[19]

The Private Security Industry Act 2001 introduced a licence requirement for all security officers working for 'contract' private security providers.[20] Candidates are screened for a possible criminal record and must have completed an approved training programme. The Security Industry Authority (SIA) is the body responsible for granting these licences (Crawford, 2008: 164-165). The SIA website shows that in September 2012 about 370,000 valid licences had been issued. The category of door supervisors is by far the biggest (more than 200,000).[21] It is difficult to assess how many licence holders are employed in public or semipublic space. The British Security Industry Association (BSIA) indicates on its website that their member companies employ 75,500 security officers.[22] Of these, it is also impossible to say how many of them are working in public or semipublic space.

19 Respondent 3 England & Wales points out that you have to work in the field of community safety to become accredited. Private security guards must therefore work in hospitals or nightlife areas, for example.

20 In-house guards are not included in this licensing regime.

21 Website of the Security Industry Authority: www.sia.homeoffice.gov.uk/Pages/licensing-stats.aspx, retrieved at 27 September 2012.

22 Website of the British Security Industry Association: www.bsia.co.uk/facts-and-figures, retrieved at 26 September 2012.

Powers and requirements for licensing

Section 7 of the Private Security Industry Act (2001) states that persons should have the skills and training necessary to perform security tasks reliably and competently. The SIA document 'Get Licensed, SIA licensing criteria' (Security Industry Authority, 2010: 17, 51-52) provides that the performance of work in the public space requires the following: private security guards must be at least eighteen years of age, must have been subject to an identity check and criminal record check, and must have completed an appropriate, SIA-approved training course. This course (which is offered by many organizations) includes components such as knowledge of the law relating to private security, how to act in an emergency, communication and reporting skills, and avoidance of personal risk.[23] Security guards do not have more powers than ordinary citizens. They can only operate as surveillance officers, just like wardens. However, they may exclude groups or individuals from the private locations they guard, under orders of the property owner (Crawford, 2008: 164).

The security guards' equipment is not defined. They are not allowed to carry attributes that can be used in violent interventions. Their uniforms are issued by the company they work for.

Recent developments

An early study by Jones and Newburn (1998) in the London borough of Wandsworth showed that almost every large building in that municipality had its own security guards. This includes not just shopping and entertainment centres, but also schools, hospitals and large offices. The few gated communities in Wandsworth also had private security guards.

Other studies show that public police officers and private security guards (including CCTV staff employed in control rooms) often work closely together.[24] The public police are frequently present in shopping malls and other mass private properties, usually to exchange data on CCTV images. The security personnel control rooms are also used by the public police, for example to track down drug dealers. The atmosphere between the two professional groups is not always good and may sometimes be hostile; guards often feel they are treated as inferiors (Norris & McCahill, 2006).

---

23 Website of the Security Industry Authority: www.sia.homeoffice.gov.uk/Pages/training-sg.aspx, retrieved at 27 September 2012.

24 In the English debate on public and private police, the work of private security guards in shopping centres is usually not called 'public'. After all, they work within private property. This view does not apply once inside large malls where municipal or other services are also located, that are not aimed at consumers but at citizens. Sometimes malls are so large that they also act as public transition space.

A study by Wakefield (2005) shows that the work of security guards in shopping malls entails many public functions, such as providing information to the police, creating risk profiles, the exclusion of (alleged) 'known criminals', and calling in the police in case of emergency. In large shopping malls the security staff have daily contact with the police, including information exchange, handing over cases, joint operations, and joint use of CCTV data. Simultaneously, the staff often gain access to personal information usually reserved for public officials (Wakefield, 2006: 403). All these functions have little to do with the protection of private property or compliance with commercial interests. Wakefield concludes that security officers today play a prominent role in public safety.
People are regularly excluded and moved on, especially juveniles. Usually this does not happen at the gate, but when the persons in question have already entered the premises. According to Wakefield, staff sometimes get involved in incidents that take place outside the centres (2005: 539).[25]
In one of the largest shopping malls in Europe, MetroCentre in Gateshead near Newcastle (6,000 employees), a team of 'community beat managers' works in a public-private partnership. The management of the shopping mall has signed an agreement with the police. The contracted police officers act as 'village bobby' in the common areas of MetroCentre.[26] Many young visitors to MetroCentre are preventively excluded. According to Crawford, deviant persons are regularly removed from malls arbitrarily and without justification (Crawford, 2011: 492-5).

A recent study of surveillance officers working in English city centre areas indicates that there were 59 Business Improvement Districts (BIDs) in 2008 (Cook, 2010). These BIDs have the job of ensuring that the public with purchasing power can find its way to the inner cities. Cook studied three districts (in Coventry, Reading, and Plymouth) in detail. The districts are urban downtown areas that include many streets. The BIDs receive regular financial contributions from the municipalities, but they also rely on contributions from shopkeepers and other businesses. The staff employed by the BIDs focus for example on cleaning, making decorations and lighting, marketing, customer familiarization, CCTV monitoring and surveillance. The staff consists of private security personnel (in-

25 Respondent 4 England & Wales points out that private security guards who are employed within shopping malls are usually instructed not to continue their work in the public space, for example, to stop and hold thieves. This might cause problems with insurance: *"Private security guards are careful with this. In this industry you do not get paid very much. Accidents are not compensated when taking place in the public space "*

26 These are hired policemen; also called paid duty officers (see a more detailed description in the chapter on Canada). Under section 9 of the Police and Magistrate's Courts Act of 1994, the police are allowed to outsource their services (see Crawford and Lister 2003). Since then, the commercial activities of the police seem to have grown considerably. In 2009, the police appear to have earned £ 17 million. See www.mirror.co.uk/news/uk-news/police-forces-making-fortune-hiring-220033, retrieved 08 January 2013.

house or contract basis), as well as wardens and PCSOs. Partly because budgets can be found only for short periods, there are frequent changes in the deployment of staff. In Plymouth security guards were replaced by PCSOs because the latter have greater enforcement powers, including the issue of fines (Cook, 2010: 467). PCSOs would be more respected by the public. In Coventry wardens are employed; they do surveillance work, including the parking lots. It is difficult to assess the extent to which these surveillance officers adjust their work to commercial purposes (Crawford, 2011).[27]

Another market segment on which security companies focus is residential area patrols. Here security guards keep an eye on residences and other buildings in return for a monthly fee (Crawford and Lister, 2003). Their activities consist of (day and night) surveillance from cars, with the guards also responding to residents' calls. Little research has been done on these developments. In England, as in many other countries, security firms devote themselves mainly to the surveillance of industrial or other properties in suburban and rural areas, but there is a tendency also to patrol in cities. In Darlington and Southampton, Sparta and Atraks, respectively, perform surveillance work in residential areas.[28] These guards also take action against antisocial behaviour (which every citizen is allowed to do). In Darlington, the police were opposed to the initiative. Police spokesmen argue that the security firm in question increases residents' fear of crime and undermines confidence in the police. The police announced they would not cooperate with these companies.[29] Another example concerns Garde UK, which offers to provide 24-hour services to the population of Essex (contribution: £1 a week).[30] The company wants to patrol in neighbourhoods with many nuisance problems and is accredited by the Essex Police. It is thus empowered to impose fines for nuisance behaviour etc.

Research by Noaks (2000 and 2008) showed that the police could experience difficulties with residential patrols carried out by security companies. The company she studied offered services both to homeowners in the private sector and tenants; the police did not consider this company a bona fide organization. There was no cooperation or exchange of information between the two, and both did their work separately from each other. The population in the area Noaks studied appeared to have more confidence in the private police. Accord-

27 One of the respondents doubted whether many private security guards are deployed in BIDs. Interview with respondent 4 England & Wales.

28 www.guardian.co.uk/society/2010/jul/28/private-security-companies-police-housing-estates, retrieved 11 January 2013.

29 http://newsvote.bbc.co.uk/mpapps/pagetools/print/news.bbc.co.uk/2/hi/programmes/politics_show/regions/north_east_and_cumbria/8564724.stm, retrieved 11 January 2013.

30 www.bbc.co.uk/news/uk-england-essex-12634162, http://www.vipsecurityservices.co.uk/Essex_Security_Firms_now_Patrol_Residential_Areas, both retrieved 11 January 2013.

ing to the researcher, the regular police had lost contact with the residents and were poorly informed about what is going on.

Exceptionally, municipalities are persuaded – sometimes in partnership – to appoint private security guards. Such an initiative emerged in York (Crawford et al., 2003). In 2003, sixteen of the twenty-two districts in York appointed security guards to conduct surveillance in the public space. As is usual with security companies, the work was done from cars. Eighty per cent of the work focused on anti-social behaviour. In 2007 the number of districts that funded these 'community rangers' was reduced to eleven, and in 2011 only two were left. According to researcher Lister this decline – besides being due to municipal budget cuts- can be explained by the following factors: the rangers have hardly any guidance; they do not meet the expectations of the population; they are difficult to approach; and cooperation with the police is poor.[31]

3.5 Relations with the police

Since the Crime and Disorder Act of 1998, each municipality is required to establish a 'Crime and Disorder Reduction Partnership' (CDRP), within which plans are drawn up to tackle crime and disorder. The plans specify how and with whom cooperation takes place and agreements are also made about the use of PCSOs, wardens and security guards (Crawford et al., 2005: 21).
Section 115 of the Crime and Disorder Act stipulates that information exchange between 'key public authorities' is permitted. In addition, data may be provided to officials who have tasks and responsibilities within the CDRP. This therefore means that information can be exchanged between police officers, wardens and security guards who are active within the same CDRP. Crawford notes that the information exchanged is often anonymized; such exchanges are regulated by protocols. The police often fail to use information collected by wardens and security guards (ibid: 75-76).
Cooperation between the partners varies greatly in different municipalities, thanks in part to the following factors: the attitude of the local Chief Constable; the extent to which the municipality has placed insecurity on the agenda; and the central government's funding regime. Cooperation is very intensive in some municipalities, and various types of surveillance and enforcement officers are working together (ibid.).

Procedures within partnerships have eased considerably since the coalition government came to power. For example, one of the respondents indicated that

31 www.law.leeds.ac.uk/assets/files/research/ccjs/stuart_lister_on_private_secuirty_patrols.pdf, retrieved 11 January 2013.

substantial deregulation had occurred within the partnerships: there are no longer any centrally imposed targets, and the selection of problematic neighbourhoods in which to target investment occurs more smoothly.[32] On the other hand, some councils say they no longer have a CDRP due to budget cuts. It could be argued that the cuts introduced by the government coalition are dismantling the architecture of the community safety partnerships.[33]
Some respondents believe that information exchange is still the major difficulty, one example being information about crime that social workers and doctors could provide. Often there is a lack of trust; the protection of clients' privacy also plays a major role. Mutatis mutandis, police officers also find it difficult to share information because, according to one of the respondents, they trust no one until they have worked with them.[34]

There is often no involvement of security guards in local partnerships (Crawford, 2007). As stated above, police and security officers usually work closely together in the large shopping malls. They also have a common interest in using CCTV images. There are mutual tensions in the neighbourhoods where security companies offer their services; the police believe that the guards have insufficient professional expertise and believe that these companies should not work in neighbourhoods where the police also operate daily (Noaks, 2000 and 2008). It is noteworthy that the Accreditation Scheme was created in 2002, but many police chiefs seem to be afraid of actually granting security guards such powers. They hesitate to deploy security guards, despite the regulation of the private security industry (White & Smith, 2009: 82-83).

3.6 Protection of citizens

The Independent Police Complaints Commission (IPCC) was established with the Police Reform Act 2002.[35] The IPCC oversees the handling of complaints by the police and sets the standards by which the police should deal with such complaints. The IPCC takes its decisions independently of the police, the government and the complainants. The commission undertakes appeal cases. Each police force has a Professional Standards Department (PSD), which is responsible for handling complaints and matters relating to the conduct of police officers within their force. Most of the complaints that the IPCC receives are passed to the PSD for further handling and resolution. The police must refer the most serious cases

32 Interview with respondent 1 England & Wales.

33 www.crimetalk.org.uk/reviews/articles/619-the-crime-and-disorder-act-overlapping-legislation-or-a-forgotten-philosophy.html, retrieved 15 April 2013.

34 Interview with respondent 6 England & Wales.

35 Part 2 of the Police Reform Act 2002.

to the IPCC and, when public interest so requires, the IPCC may decide to initiate an independent investigation.[36]
In the period 2010/2011 there were 1,016 complaints about the behaviour of PCSOs, which is 3% of the total number of complaints against the police in the period (total: 37,189) (Independent Police Complaints Commission, 2011). This perhaps gives a distorted picture of dissatisfaction with the actions of PCSOs. PCSOs are supposed to call in the help of police officers in problem situations, and the police officers will then take over the conflicts. Initial dissatisfaction with the actions of PCSOs could therefore be visible in the complaints about the actions of police officers.
In regard to security guards, citizens can lodge their complaints with the company for which they work. Complaints may also be filed on the SIA website. If citizens are not satisfied, they can go to court.[37]

3.7 Debate

The debate over public surveillance officers in England & Wales currently focuses largely on the steep budget cuts and their possible implications for frontline work. Right-wing politicians call for further privatization. The Policy Exchange thinktank, for instance, favours the idea that relatively expensive sworn constables should be freed of all kinds of office tasks to be able to devote themselves to fighting crime.[38] The office tasks could be outsourced as far as possible to security companies. The police would therefore operate more efficiently and visibly (also Loveday, 2013).
The question is what the effect of personnel reduction will have on frontline work. One of the respondents believes that neighbourhood policing will come under severe pressure from the cuts. His expectation is that many officers and PCSOs will disappear from the safer neighbourhood teams. The reassurance function will lose its importance, especially as the number of wardens is also reduced. According to this interviewee, municipalities would do well to build up their own enforcement services. In addition, municipalities should be given more powers to provide their own enforcement officers.[39]
Another respondent also points out that the formula of safer neighbourhood teams will come under pressure by the cuts, which he believes will be impossible

36 Website of the Independent Police Complaints Commission: www.ipcc.gov.uk, retrieved 21 September 2012.
37 Interviews with respondents 3 and 4 England & Wales.
38 www.thetimes.co.uk/tto/business/industries/publicsector/article3345226.ece, retrieved 14 March 2013
39 Interview with respondent 5 England & Wales.

to maintain. The tasks of community engagement and the problem-solving approach will be imperilled.[40]

Another topical issue is the role of private security companies in the public space. All respondents emphasize that the population still has a lot of confidence in the public police. They state that there are great reservations about giving more powers to security guards operating in the streets. One of the respondents, a former Chief Constable, said:

> 'Private security guards do not walk on the streets and indeed this should not happen. Over my dead body! (...) That will really confuse the public. On the street there should be no doubt officers who are responsible. I think that private parties also have no desire to do this. (...) That they will take over more back-office functions seems no problem to me."[41]

Nevertheless, entrepreneurs, retailers and businesses often call for more private security guards in inner cities, pointing out that the police do nothing about anti-social behaviour.[42]
Simultaneously, there seems to be dissatisfaction about the role of the public police in suburban and sparsely populated rural areas, where the police do not maintain a very visible presence. If private security guards are hired, this dissatisfaction might further increase because homeowners think they have to pay twice. Where residents and homeowners pay for the services of security companies, the public police can almost never succeed. There is also the chance that homeowners might play off the police against the security guards, or vice versa. Be that as it may, the public police have a defensive attitude to security companies that offer services in the public space (Noaks, 2008).
After the 'G4S fiasco' during the Olympic Games, the public's expectations of private organizations decreased significantly. The PCC candidates were starkly divided on this subject in the police commissioner elections (November 2012). Many candidates have explicitly opposed privatization and contracting out of police tasks.[43]
Finally, there is a debate about the vital role of the PCSOs and the lack of sworn officers in the streets. This discussion is also related to budget cuts. For example, several hundred police officers have lost their jobs in South Yorkshire. Subsequently the PCSOs were given more powers and are now acting as local beat

40 Interview with respondent 7 England & Wales.
41 Interview with respondent 7 England & Wales.
42 www.liverpooldailypost.co.uk/liverpool-news/regional-news/2008/04/01/call-for-zero-tolerance-security-patrols-for-entire-city-centre-99623-20699949, retrieved 11 January 2013.
43 www.guardian.co.uk/politics/blog/2012/nov/14/police-commissioner-contracts-privatisation-elections/print, retrieved 15 April 2013

officers. They are the first point of contact for the public in the streets. According to some policymakers this development would virtually condemn the police to a more reactive role behind the scenes. This, they claim, cannot be the intention. That would mean the end of the 'bobbies on the beat'. Moreover, the public will be further alienated from the police if they only see PCSOs. Some police spokesmen deny that sworn constables would no longer be visible on the streets.[44]

3.8 Conclusion

In recent decades a fragmented landscape of surveillance and enforcement officers has arisen in England & Wales. Nevertheless, in cities the PCSOs largely determine the streetscape. They are the public face of the police organization and are by far the most important group of officials with whom the public has regular contact. Thus, in England & Wales a 'police solution' for the regulation of nuisance, anti-social behaviour and petty crime has grown. The police are still of the opinion that this is the right direction. Generally, they emphasize the declining figures for subjective insecurity and increased confidence in the police. The PCSOs are the vehicle for a safer neighbourhood and the people seem to appreciate that commitment. To what extent the use of PCSOs will remain intact in the future is difficult to say.

The findings on the deployment of wardens are broadly positive. The political climate, however, seems unfavourable to these go-betweens. Many municipalities do not want to spend (more) money on them, or they prefer officers with enforcement powers. The special constables may, in these times of austerity, develop as a relatively inexpensive vehicle to keep surveillance officers on the street.

The number of private security guards has grown strongly in recent decades. They are prepared to offer their services also in the public space, but still seem to have few opportunities for solid growth in that domain, probably not even within the Business Improvement Districts. The police still have a reserved attitude to security guards in frontline work.

44 www.telegraph.co.uk/news/uknews/crime/9201760/Beat-bobbies-to-be-replaced-by-plastic-police.html; www.guardian.co.uk/uk/2012/apr/13/south-yorkshire-defends-pcso-plans?INTCMP=SRCH; www.telegraph.co.uk/news/uknews/2231521/Police-on-the-beat-could-disappear-in-a-decade.html, all retrieved 11 January 2013.

4 Austria

There are two very important elements to an understanding of plural policing in Austria. First, Austria (with a population of 8.3 million) has a complex administrative structure. As a federal state it consists of four administrative layers: the federation (the national level of the *Bund*), nine provinces (*Länder*), 80 districts (*Bezirke*) and 2,354 municipalities (*Gemeinde*). The lowest layer, the municipalities, is fairly small in scale. If Vienna is disregarded (more than one in four Austrians live there), Austrian municipalities have an average size of about 2,500 inhabitants. This complex administrative structure has several important consequences for the Austrian police system.

Secondly, Austria has a relatively strong legalistic culture. The documents examined for this study and the interviews conducted suggest that in this country the theme of plural policing is (almost) exclusively interpreted and analysed in legal terms. Moreover, belief in the state and in hierarchical relationships is relatively strong. The impacts of a neo-liberal discourse (with its strong emphasis on the importance of market and market mechanisms and on the need to roll back the state) and of a general social and cultural shift from a hierarchical to a more egalitarian society (De Swaan, 1982) have been much less dominant in Austria, certainly if compared with the Netherlands, for instance, which has experienced such radical, even drastic cultural changes, especially since the 1970s.

Although both public and private non-police providers of policing have also gained a position in the public space in Austria over the past ten to fifteen years, hardly any social scientific (criminological, sociological or public administration) research has been done on the introduction and implementation of these forms of policing.[1] Moreover, most of the few studies in Austria are by legal scholars. These studies often focus on fundamental legal issues, such as the compatibility of non-police policing bodies with constitutional principles in Austria or with human rights.

1 Interviews with respondents 4 and 6 Austria. The only exceptions that were found are two academic legal publications by Fuchs (2005 and 2012) on private security, both of which also contain empirical data.

The structure of this chapter is as follows. First, there is a brief sketch of the police system in Austria (4.1). Next, the municipal wardens are described, who made their appearance in Austria about ten years ago (4.2). Because the backgrounds, organization and position of these municipal wardens differ from city to city, the municipal wardens in two cities (Graz and Linz) are discussed in more detail (4.3). The role of private security in public space in Austria is then considered (4.4), followed by a brief analysis of the relations between the public wardens and private guards on the one hand and the regular police on the other (4.5). The final section (4.6) contains some concluding remarks and reviews the complex system of plural policing in Austria.

4.1 Police system

Federal police

Austria has two types of police organization (*Wachkörper*), namely the federal police force (which is by far the largest) and the (much smaller) municipal police forces.[2] The three national police forces that existed in the country merged in 2005: the Federal Security Corps (*Bundessicherheitswache)* (responsible for policing in the fourteen large cities), the Federal Gendarmerie (*Bundesgendarmerie)* (working outside the major cities) and the Corps of Criminal Investigators (*Kriminalbeamtenkorps)* (a federal police organization with a criminal investigation task). These three organizations were incorporated into the Federal Police (*Bundespolizei*). In September 2012, the Federal Police was once again radically restructured. Since then, new authorities of the Federal Police have been established in the nine provinces (*Länder)*. Each provincial division is under the command of a Provincial Police Director (*Landespolizeidirektion)* and has a number of divisions, such as traffic monitoring, criminal investigation, or what is called operational tasks. Most of the approximately 20,000 employees of the Federal Police are employed in one of more than nine hundred (local or regional) police districts (*Polizeiinspektionen)*.

In contrast to other federal countries (such as Germany, Switzerland, Canada or the United States), Austria has no (autonomous) police forces at the level of the provinces (Wenda, 2013). The Security Police Act (*Sicherheitspolizeigesetz)* is a federal law. However, because the police also execute laws that may differ by province (*Land*), the overall powers of the Federal Police vary by province, to some degree.[3] In addition, there is a strict legal distinction between the tasks of the

2 According to the Federal Constitution (*Bundes-Verfassungsgesetz)* (art. 78d (1)) *Wachkörper* are uniformed organizations with a general (police) task structured as military units.

3 Interviews with respondents 3 and 4 Austria.

Federal Police and those of the municipality. According to the Austrian constitution (*Bundes-Verfassungsgesetz*), the Federal Police cannot deal with cases that concern the local administrative security (*örtliche Sicherheitspolizei*).[4] This is defined as the responsibility of the municipality alone.[5]

Municipal police

In addition to the federal police, Austria also has municipal police forces. Different terms are used, such as municipal police bodies (*Gemeindewachkörper*), municipal security police (*Gemeindesicherheitswachen*), or city security police (*Städtische Sicherheitswache*).

These local police forces are founded according to the Austrian constitution,[6] which gives the municipalities the space to create their own police force, although they require permission from the federal government to do so.[7] In principle, municipalities can have fully-fledged police forces that have the complete range of police powers at their disposal. In practice, however, the powers of the municipal force may differ, depending on the size of the force, among other things. The tasks of the large municipal forces may also include criminal investigation, in addition to service to citizens, enforcement of local administrative regulations and social order, and the enforcement of parking regulations (Wenda 2011a and 2011b).

A municipal organization with surveillance and enforcement tasks can only be viewed as a police force (*Wachkörper*) as defined by the Austrian constitution if it has a complement of a certain minimum size. In practice, the size of the municipal police forces varies considerably, from 45 employees (in Baden) to only a few in some small municipalities in the western part of Austria.

It is legally prohibited for municipalities in Austria to share a municipal police force. Such a municipal force should be subordinate to the authority of the mayor of the municipality. The officers working in this force are employees of the municipality (Wenda, 2013).

Municipal governments have to fund the municipal force from their own resources. The exception here is Vorarlberg, the most Western province (*Land*) of Austria, where the provincial government contributes to the funding of municipal police forces (Wenda, 2011a).[8]

4 *Bundes-Verfassungsgesetz*, Article 10, (1) 7: '*The Federation has powers of legislation and execution in the following matters: the maintenance of peace, order and security including the extension of primary assistance in general, but excluding local public safety matters.*'

5 *Bundes-Verfassungsgesetz*, Article 15 (2) and Article 118 (1) 3. Also: Neuhofer (1998), Stolzlechner & Horvath (2009). The interviewees proved to have different opinions about the correct interpretation of this formal arrangement. See below in this chapter.

6 *Bundes-Verfassungsgesetz* Article 15 (2), 118 (3) en 118a.

7 *Bundes-Verfassungsgesetz*, Article 118 (8).

8 Interviews with respondents 3 and 4 Austria.

Municipal police are obliged to cooperate with the Federal Police. In practice there is often some division of labour, for example with the municipal force focusing on local issues and the Federal Police doing the criminal investigation of the more serious cases. In some cases they share a common public telephone number and a single emergency room.
The Federal Police and the municipal forces usually do not differ very much in their uniforms and equipment. Although the municipalities are free to decide on the style of uniform their police officers wear, they often wear uniforms that are more or less similar to that of the Federal Police, the main difference being in the coat of arms on their uniforms; for the Federal Police this is the federal eagle, for the municipal forces it may be the municipal coat of arms.

The Austrian constitution (article 78d (2)) forbids the establishment of a municipal police force in municipalities with a Provincial Police Directorate in its territory.[9] This prohibition dates from the 1920s, a period of great political unrest, fierce conflicts and the rise of National Socialism in Austria. The present-day motivation is the fear that (as happened in those years in Austria) police forces in a certain area might be set up against each other and/or play an explicit political role (Wenda, 2013).[10] This legal prohibition implies that the large Austrian cities (like Vienna, Linz, Graz, Innsbruck or Salzburg) are not permitted to establish their own municipal police force. This mainly relates to *'Statutarstädte'* (statutory cities), which means those cities that also have the formal powers of a district. In Austria the local administration of these cities is called the magistrature (*Magistrat*).

Before the Second World War there were still hundreds of municipalities that had their own police force, but the number has declined significantly since then. In the 1980s there were still more than 80 municipal forces, while the number had dropped to 45 by the late 1990s. At present only 37 Austrian municipalities still have their own police force (Wenda, 2013).[11] These municipal police forces are mainly to be found in medium-sized municipalities and in the provinces of Tyrol and Vorarlberg.[12]

9 This article states (literally translated): *'No other territorial authority may, within the territorial sphere of competence of a Federal Police Directorate, to which a Federal Police force is attached, set up or maintain a constabulary.'* Until September 2012 this involved the presence in the municipality of a District Federal Police Directorate (*Bundespolizeidirektion*).

10 Interviews with respondents 4 and 6 Austria.

11 Interviews with respondents 3 and 4 Austria.

12 The interviewees do not entirely agree about the factors that contributed to the concentration of municipal police forces in Tyrol and Vorarlberg. One of them thinks that regional ambitions for more autonomy and a general aversion to the central government in Vienna may have contributed. In contrast, another respondent believes that this unlikely because the concentration of municipal police forces in those provinces had only arisen in recent decades, at a time when the ambition for more autonomy had become less urgent.

Although Austrian municipal governments often have a distinct need for more police in their territory, the number of municipal forces is still declining. The interviewees mentioned several factors that may have contributed to this. First, municipal governments must fund a municipal police force entirely from their own resources (with the exception of Vorarlberg, where the Province partially contributes to the costs). Moreover, in some cases the municipal police forces (partly due to their small size) simply do not meet the requirements of a fully-fledged force. Finally, in such a case it may be more attractive for municipalities to contract a private security company. Although private security officers in Austria have no formal police powers, they are still able to meet the need for a more visible uniformed surveillance in the public space. Generally this is also substantially cheaper for the municipal governments. Moreover, it creates the possibility of a more flexible organization, the size of which may be customized, according to the changing demands and circumstances of the moment.[13]

4.2 Public Order Services and City Guard Departments

Municipal wardens

Since 2007, Austrian municipal organizations have been created that are responsible for surveillance and (to a lesser degree) enforcement in the public space. These organizations are known by various names, including Public Order Service (*Ordnungsdienst)* and City Guard Department (*Stadtwache).* The first municipal authority to set up such an organization was Graz, in 2007. The city of Linz and other Austrian cities followed. It was from that time onward that the position and working methods of these new municipal providers of surveillance and enforcement took shape.

The formal powers of these organizations vary slightly in the provinces and municipalities, but they are usually quite limited. In some cases the officers of these municipal services may request a citizen to show an ID. In a few cases (see below in this chapter for more details) they may impose an administrative fine. Generally speaking, the powers of these municipal wardens do not go beyond the usual rights that any citizen in Austria has, the so-called *Jedermannsrecht* (Everyman's right). This includes, among other things, the right to self-defence/ emergency assistance (*Notwehr/Nothilfe)* and the right to provisional (citizen) arrest (*vorläufige Festnahme*) awaiting the arrival of the police.[14] Apart from this

13 Interviews with respondents 1, 3 and 4 Austria. This is relevant especially in the Austrian tourist (ski) areas, where there may be a great seasonal variation in the need for surveillance in the public space.

14 Interviews with respondents 4 and 5 Austria.

Everyman's right, there is no legal basis in Austria that provides special powers to these Public Order Services, at either the federal or the provincial level.[15]
For this reason it is often strongly emphasized that the tasks and powers of these municipal services should not be confused with those of the police. According to the Austrian legal standards, these municipal services do not perform real police work (Wenda, 2011b: 14), a view that is strongly related to the dominant formal, rather narrow interpretation of 'police' in Austria.
The tasks of these municipal providers (in addition to the provision of services and information to citizens and shopkeepers) include surveillance in the public space, the enforcement of local administrative rules and regulations (including those relating to stray dogs, making music in public and begging), the maintenance of public order, and the prevention of various forms of disorder and nuisance. In some cases these municipal wardens perform their work mainly at certain times (for example evenings or weekends) and/or locations (like shopping centres or nightlife areas).
In principle the Austrian Arms Act allows individual employees of these municipal services to apply successfully for a firearms licence, implying that they might carry a weapon during their work (Wenda, 2013). However, with the exception of the city of Innsbruck, where the municipal guards carry pepper spray, the municipal governments have decided that their wardens and guards should not be equipped with batons, handcuffs and/or firearms. Normally these municipal guards and wardens should do their work by maintaining a recognizable presence in the public space, addressing citizens and reporting problems to the police and other municipal departments.
The municipal guards of the Public Order Services wear uniforms during their work on the streets. The similarity of their uniforms to police uniforms differs between the municipalities.
The position and organization of these municipal services also differ. In some cases they are a department of the municipal administration (or the *Magistrat*), which may be combined with other municipal enforcement tasks; in other cases it is a semi-autonomous organization.
No precise data are available on the number of municipalities in Austria that have a Public Order Service. It may be assumed that about ten to fifteen cities have such wardens or guards. In most cases these municipalities are statutory cities or municipalities with (until September 2012) a District Federal Police Directorate.[16]

Social backgrounds

The introduction of Public Order Services in Austria has to be understood in the context of both major social changes, as well as the specific legal constellation of

15 A partial exception exists for Styria (*Steiermark*) (see later in this chapter).
16 See section 4.1.

the country. In seeking to understand this pluralization of policing in Austria, most attention has been paid to the legal circumstances, but social changes are probably more important. It would otherwise not be easy to understand why in Austria, despite its specific legal context, developments in local policing and security are so similar to those in other European countries. That is why we first discuss a number of relevant social developments, before looking at some of the legal aspects.

As in many other European countries, political attention for problems of public safety grew strongly in Austria in the 1990s (although the country had a relatively low incidence of crime in those years). The FPÖ (Freedom Party of Austria) in particular, a far-right political party that gained prominence in the 1990s, put a strong emphasis on public safety as a major issue, propagating tough measures to fight crime and disorder.[17] The FPÖ was especially strong in Graz, which makes it easier to understand why the first initiatives for a Public Order Service were taken there. More recently, the FPÖ seems to have become more ambivalent about these municipal guards and wardens.[18]

For the past twenty years in Austria, too, public security has increasingly been defined as not the responsibility of the police and criminal justice agencies alone, but as an area in which other agencies should also contribute, although this development is still more modest than in many other European countries (cf. Crawford, 1997; Terpstra, 2008). Even though in Austria there is still a strong focus on the state, especially in policing and security, a shift from 'government to governance' can be noted in the management of crime and disorder here too (Fuchs, 2005 and 2012). For example, according to Stolzlechner and Horvath (2009: 67) Austria has shifted towards:

> 'a new division of labour between the state, municipal government and private agencies in relation to increased individual and shared responsibilities in risk management.'

In addition, for about the last ten years the distance between the (federal) police and local communities and local governments has been gradually widening. This development is often understood as a consequence of the 2005 reform of the Austrian police, resulting in a single Federal Police force. In the years following this reform, 120 mainly small Gendarmerie police stations were closed and police units were merged, the aim being to enhance police effectiveness. As a result, many citizens began to perceive a 'security vacuum'. Municipal governments in particular were confronted with these negative developments. Many Austrian municipal governments tried to create a solution to the resulting gap in local sur-

17 Interviews with respondents 3 and 6 Austria. FPÖ = *Freiheitliche Partei Österreichs* (Freedom Party of Austria).

18 See section 4.3.

veillance and enforcement in the public space. Their main strategy was to try to strengthen the surveillance and (if possible) enforcement of local rules and regulations (*ortspolizeilicher Verordnungen*), which was mainly funded from their own municipal resources. This also implied that administrative law became more important for local security. These elements have contributed to a significant change ('paradigm shift') in Austria, where the police are no longer the only actor in this field, but have been supplemented by other non-police actors (Stolzlechner en Horvath, 2009: 77).

According to one of the interviewees, the withdrawal of the police at the federal level had in fact already started earlier. As early as 2002, there were important reforms in the then federal police forces. The managements of the three forces were merged, resulting in a more top-down police organization. It was assumed that with the availability of new ICT, a strongly centralized police organization became feasible for the first time. Following the discourse of the new managerialism (Terpstra & Trommel, 2009), a strict system of performance management was introduced. As a result, the priorities of police work shifted from the local to the national level, the latter mainly being devoted to fighting crime. Less attention was paid to local priorities, such as the visible presence of police officers on the streets. According to one interviewee, this development paved the way for the 2005 police reform, which served to reinforced the process. The result is now a greater distance between the (federal) police and the municipal level. The interviewee even speaks of *"a new gap within the police, between the top and the street level"*.[19]

Municipal governments in Austria have tried to compensate for the resulting gap in local surveillance and enforcement. In addition to the Public Order Services, two other strategies are used. First, some municipal governments deploy members of their own staff for surveillance tasks on the streets. For example, in 2010 Eisenstadt and Salzburg established so-called Mobile Assistance Troops (*Mobile Unterstützungs Truppe*, also known as MUT). In these cities, some municipal employees, in addition to their regular job, were deployed as a Public Order Service (*Ordnungsdienst*). Members of the MUT were to conduct surveillance in the public space, promote peace and social order, and report potential safety risks and social disorder. In the city of Eisenstadt these MUT officers wear a special uniform while performing their work. The uniform looks somewhat like a police uniform.[20] Secondly, there are municipalities that decided to hire private security officers, an issue that is dealt with in more detail in section 4.4.

19 Interview respondent 3 Austria. This analysis is confirmed by the developments in the city of Linz (see section 4.3). One of the other interviewees thinks there is no relation between the 2005 police reform and the growing withdrawal by the police from the local level.

20 ORF.at, '*Eisenstadt bekommt Ordnungsdienst "MUT"*', 6 May 2010, http://bglvl.orf.at/stories/441002, retrieved 22 August 2012. After long debates in Salzburg in November 2010 the plan actually started with six employees (derived from: www.meinbezirk.at/salzburg-stadt/politik/nur-wenig-gebuehrenerhoehung-d37320.html, retrieved 22 November 2012.

Legal context

Some specific legal factors also contributed to the introduction of Public Order Services in Austria. These legal factors have imposed some specific forms on plural policing in the country.

In accordance with Article 78d (2) of the Austrian constitution. mentioned above, municipalities with a Provincial Police Directorate in their territory are not permitted to establish their own municipal police force. This legal prohibition has some serious implications for the larger cities in Austria. If local governments in these cities feel that more surveillance and enforcement in the public space is needed (because the Federal Police do not pay sufficient attention to it), they cannot create their own municipal police force. The only option the municipal governments have is to create a Public Order Service (an organization without police powers) (Wenda, 2013).
This legal regulation may be difficult for outsiders to understand; it has even caused some debate in Austria itself. For example, in 2012 the leader of the ÖVP (Austrian People's Party) in the Parliament of the province of Upper Austria (*Oberösterreich*) proposed to strike out Article 78d (2) of the constitution. Such a decision would make it possible for the governments of the larger cities in Austria to have their own municipal police force, i.e. one with police powers. In this politician's view, this would be much better than the *'second-rate solution'* of municipal wardens and guards who lack any specific powers.[21] In the end the proposal was not adopted.[22] The fear that different police forces may come into a conflict, based as it is on Austrian history, means that Article 78d (2) still appears to remain uncontested dogma.
Apart from that, even if such cities were to have the legal potential to establish their own municipal police force, many of them would probably refrain from doing so, the main reason being that they would have to fund such a local force entirely from their own resources.[23] This may be one of the reasons why the political debate on abolishing Article 78d (2) has not been taken very seriously.[24]

In accordance with articles 15 (2) and 118 (6) of the Austrian constitution. municipal governments are entitled to establish an executive service for the enforcement

21 OÖNachrichten, 15 May 2012: www.nachrichten.at/nachrichten/politik/innenpolitik/art385,886236, retrieved 30 August 2012; OÖNachrichten, 7 April 2012: www.nachrichten.at/nachrichten/politik/landespolitik/art383,857738, retrieved 30 August 2012.

22 Interview with respondent 3 Austria.

23 Moreover, to establish a municipal police force the municipal governments would have to meet several conditions, such as the size of the force.

24 Interview with respondent 4 Austria. In his view, partly because of the financial burden, many Austrian municipalities have closed down their municipal police force in recent decades; this also means that a change of art 78 (2) has low political priority.

of local administrative regulations (such as a ban on dogs without a leash, or prohibiting the consumption of alcohol in public).[25] However, two legal complications arise in this case.
First, these articles do not confer any more specific powers on a municipal Public Order Service than those of the Everyman's right. In 2007 the Surveillance Agency Act (*Aufsichtsorgangesetz)* was introduced in the province of Styria (*Steiermark*). This Act gives a stronger legal basis to the Public Order Service in the city of Graz. With the introduction of this act, wardens of the municipal Public Order Service in Graz have powers that include the arrest of a person to establish his/her identity, in certain circumstances the seizure of goods, and the imposition of an administrative fine (*Organstrafverfügung*) for certain infringements, on behalf of the competent administrative authority.[26] The other Austrian provinces do not have a similar legal basis for the municipal Public Order Services: here the municipal wardens have only the powers of the Everyman's right, which every Austrian citizen has.[27]

Secondly, the legal relationship between the (exclusive) jurisdiction of the Federal Police and the municipality (*Magistrat*) plays an important role here. In Austria the legal principle states that the police may only act on the basis of the Security Police Act (*Sicherheitspolizeigesetz*). Any other task that the police might carry out would first require a legal basis. According to this principle, the enforcement of municipal administrative rules and regulations (*Ortspolizeilicher Verordnungen),* including the policing of social disorder, is not defined as a proper police task. *On the other hand,* municipal government in Austria is held to be legally responsible for the enforcement of municipal administrative rules and regulations (including the policing of social disorder). However, municipal workers do not have the specific power to enforce these local regulations, such as detaining a person or checking someone's identity (Stolzlechner & Horvath, 2009: 78). In practice this may produce a stalemate. Stolzlechner and Horvath (2009) assume that this deadlock can only be resolved in one of two ways. First, it may be decided that the police and the municipal wardens of the Public Order Service undertake joint patrols. In this way the limitations in the powers of the municipal warden may be compensated by the powers of the police (and vice versa). Secondly, as in Styria, an amendment to the Surveillance Agency Act could create the room for

25 Article 118 (6), (version of 5 June 2012) reads: *'The municipality is entitled in matters pertaining to its own sphere of competence to issue on its own initiative local police ordinances for the prevention of imminently to be expected or existent nuisances interfering with local communal life as well as to declare non-compliance with them an administrative contravention. Such ordinances may not violate existent laws and ordinances of the Federation and Land.'*

26 Steiermärkisches Aufsichtsorgangesetz, paragraph 7, 1-2 StAOG (Stammfassung: LGBl. Nr. 95/2007 (XV. GPStLT RV EZ 1497/1 AB EZ 1497/4).

27 See section 4.3 for an exception in the city of Linz.

a municipal department that has the power to enforce the municipal administrative rules and regulations.[28]

Seen from an international perspective this is a rather remarkable legal construct. Empirical studies in different countries have shown that in practice a considerable part of police work consists of social service and the maintenance of peace and order (Bittner, 1970; Punch & Naylor, 1973; Verwee, 2009; Reiner, 2010). Following the Austrian legal construct just mentioned, the local management of social order in particular would not be considered to be police work. Some of the interviewees wonder whether, despite this legalistic tradition, the Austrian police would in the past still have had this much broader role in practice. They feel that the police have withdrawn only quite recently, using this principle as an argument (or, in the view of some, as an excuse).[29]
Apart from this, at least legally, a segregated form of policing is assumed in Austria, rather than an integrated one. The question that arises is which underlying factors and arguments contribute to this strict distinction between two forms of policing (the first by the police, the second by local authorities)? One of the interviewees referred to a predominant view of police work in Austria. In this view, police work is largely equated with the use of coercion. However, the imposition of a fine is not defined as a form of coercion and for that reason the municipal government is permitted to do this. According to the prevailing view, the police should not be involved in the enforcement of local administrative rules, because then there is a serious risk that the police will use coercive means even for such a petty infringement as a citizen mowing his lawn on Sunday morning (an activity that is not permitted in many Austrian municipalities). In the event the police were to try to enforce such a prohibition, it is assumed that it might easily risk escalation. In principle, the grass-mowing citizen can be repeatedly fined for his rule-breaking every Sunday, but the infringement is still not seen as so serious that coercion (and thus policing) would be appropriate.[30]

In Austria this legal, strict separation between the enforcement responsibilities of the municipal authorities and those of the police seem to be generally accepted as a given fact (also among the interviewees). Apparently this does not apply for some politicians, given the recurrent calls to give the municipal Public Order Services more police powers.
For the sake of completeness, one of the interviewees has an interpretation that differs somewhat from the predominant Austrian view of this issue. He believes

28 Interviews with respondents 1, 3, 4 and 5 Austria.

29 Interviews with respondents 5 and 6 Austria.

30 Interview with respondent 3 Austria. This differs considerably from Bittner's (1970) view that the police may use coercive means if necessary, but that good policing is characterized by the avoidance of violence as far as possible (cf. Terpstra, 2012b).

that although the police may only act on the basis of the Security Police Act, this does not imply that they do not also have a responsibility for the enforcement of the local social order. He is therefore inclined to agree with the view that the strict legal separation is mainly an excuse for the Austrian police to withdraw from local issues.[31]

4.3 Public Order Services in Graz and Linz

The origin and organization of the Public Order Services, their tasks and the ways they operate in practice, vary from city to city. This section focuses on two of these Public Order Services, namely those in Graz and in Linz. These two Public Order Services are the most frequently debated in Austria and often serve as examples for other cities.

Graz

In May 2002 in the city of Graz (the capital of the province of Styria, with about 300,000 inhabitants) the Citizen Union for Protection and Security *(Verein der Bürger für Schutz und Sicherheit)* (also known as the Graz Vigilante Force *(Grazer Bürgerwehr)*) was founded. The union's goal was the promotion of safety 'in both *ideal, and material respect'*, 'to strengthen the *awareness of measures to improve the safety and quality of life'*, especially with regard to 'crime, the *protection against disasters and the defence of the country'*. From the outset, the Citizen Union was closely affiliated with the far right political party FPÖ. The Graz Vigilante stated it wanted to fight against *'festering drug and street crime, ruthless bike pirates, people who* harass *travellers on the tram, vandalism and uncontrollable events in the parks.'* The very first public action of the Graz Vigilante provoked a great deal of controversy and criticism, not only locally, but also nationally. The members of this uniformed group, equipped with pepper spray and video cameras, decided to patrol in the direct neighbourhood of a bilingual international school in Graz. However, the school's students did not feel protected, but threatened by the presence of the Graz Vigilante. Opponents feared that persons of African descent, living in the neighbourhood, would be victims of the Graz Vigilante. Tensions grew even further when the mass media reported that a nationally well-known former SS member, also the chairman of the extreme right-wing *Kameradschaft IV* (an association of SS veterans), was also a member of the Graz Vigilante. Subsequently the school principal, the Police Director (*Polizeidirektor*) of Graz, the Minister of the Interior, the Federal Chancellor and others voiced their strong opposition to this initiative (Fuchs, 2005: 239-243).

31 Interview with respondent 6 Austria. He refers to Article 27.1 of the Security Police Act: *'The security authorities have the obligation of enforcement in public places.'*

Initially the Graz Vigilante tried to move on to another area. However, in 2003 (after the FPÖ had lost heavily in local elections), the Graz Vigilante disappeared from the public arena (Hemmer & Bauer, 2003).

Although this citizens' initiative came to an end, new initiatives along similar lines were soon to emerge in Graz. After a great deal of preparation and debate, in December 2007 the Public Order Service (*Ordnungswache Graz)* was established as a department of the municipal organization (*Magistrat).* The aim of this service was to promote surveillance in the public space and the enforcement of municipal rules and regulations. This was to contribute '*to a cleaner and more orderly city*'. The Public Order Service was to perform activities that would otherwise not be done at all because the police were said to have no resources available any longer.[32] As mentioned before, Article 78d (2) of the Austrian constitution prohibited municipal authorities like that in Graz from establishing their own municipal police force. It was for that reason that the Surveillance Agency Act (*Aufsichtsorgangesetz)* was introduced in the province of Styria in late 2007. This legal change permitted Graz to establish a municipal Public Order Service having some formal powers. Officers of the municipal Public Order Service in Graz are formally entitled to arrest a citizen to establish his/her identity, issue a warning, file a report and impose an administrative fine (*Organstrafverfügung*) in case of infringements such as dog dirt and discarding cigarettes in the street: € 10; cycling in parks and feeding the pigeons: € 30; begging and the violation of 'decency rules' (Anstandsverletzung): € 35. In addition, the officers of the Graz municipal Public Order Service should act against violations of municipal rules and regulations, such as the Clean Streets Regulation (*Strassenreinhalteverordnung),* the Parks and Public Gardens Regulation (*Grünanlagenverordnung)*, the Street Music Regulation (*Strassenmusikverordnung*), and enforce regulations such as those regarding shopping trolleys, outdoor cafés, opening hours of bars, and the use of alcoholic beverages by minor persons.[33]

Officers of the Graz Public Order Service wear a black uniform with '*Ordnungswache*' imprinted. They must have a clearly visible service logo and on request they must show their service identity card. The Graz municipal Public Order Service has its own cars (clearly recognizable to the public: silver with a blue stripe on the side, with a blue flashing light). The municipal Public Order Service officers are not armed. This fits with the frequently mentioned premise that members of Graz Public Order Service should not be seen as police officers.

In 2010 the Graz Public Order Service suffered severe budget cuts. Mainly for financial reasons, the original aim of a service of twenty wardens was abandoned. At that time the service only had a workforce of twelve. In that year, too, there was some debate about restricting the service's work domain. For instance,

32 For example, Die Presse, '*Grazer Ordnungswache ab Morgen im Einsatz*', 30 November 2007.

33 The *Ordnungsdienst Magistrat Graz*: www.graz.at/cms/beitrag/10124599/2548540, retrieved 12 September 2012 and 23 November 2012.

the Mayor of Graz suggested that the Public Order Service should only carry out surveillance in the parks. Once again (and not for the first time) there was an insistence that the police should pay more attention to surveillance and enforcement tasks in the public space.[34]

Two years on there is still great uncertainty about the Graz Public Order Service. In September 2012 it was proposed to incorporate the Public Order Service into the Graz Parking Service *(Grazer Parkraum Service)*. This would result in a more flexible organization. A stricter division was also made between the Public Order Service and the police. In the near future, for instance, officers of the Graz Public Order Service will no longer be deployed to police night-time disorders in the popular nightlife area *Univiertel*. This is now (once again) considered the proper task of the police.[35]

From the early days, the Public Order Service in Graz has been a highly sensitive political issue. Not only in Graz, but also nationally this service continues to be associated with the far-right FPÖ. This may be the result of the original association of the Public Order Service with the former Graz Vigilante, as well as the fact that the introduction of the Public Order Service was in part based on an FPÖ proposal.

Linz

Early 2009 a proposal was launched in the city of Linz (the capital of the province of Upper Austria, with about 193,000 inhabitants) to establish a Public Order Service (*Ordnungsdienst)*. The Graz Public Order Service was seen as an example. The municipal service actually started in late 2010.

Even the initial proposals for a Public Order Service prompted sharp political conflicts in Linz. The original proposal was made by the (conservative) Austrian People's Party (ÖVP). The right-wing FPÖ in the city thought that the proposal was not radical enough and preferred more (municipal) police with more powers for a tougher approach to crime and disorder. At first the local Social-Democratic Party of Austria (SPÖ) was ambivalent about this proposal, but agreed in the end. The much smaller local left-wing parties in Linz, the Green Party and the (communist) KPÖ, as well as the local Socialist Youth fiercely opposed the introduction of what they called a 'parallel police' (*Parallelpolizei)* with the political slogan 'no substitute sheriffs!' (*keine Ersatz-Sheriffs!)*. They did not see any need for such a municipal organization, which would have no powers and would only be

34 Kleine Zeitung, *Graz pfeift Ordnungswache zurück und stärkt Polizei*, www.kleinezeitung.at/steiermark/2569046/graz-pfeift-ordnungswache-zurueck-staerkt-polizei.story, 23 November 2010, retrieved 12 September 2012.

35 E-mail from respondent 4 Austria, 15 September 2012.

able to focus on 'nonsense offences'. According to these parties, tax revenue could better be spent on more worthwhile goals.[36]

In Linz the Public Order Service is incorporated as a limited liability company (LLC),[37] which is fully owned by the Linz municipal administration (*Magistrat*). The managing directors of this organization have a certain autonomy, but must operate within the established policy framework. Every quarter they have to account for their work to the supervisory board, established by the municipal council of Linz.[38]

The decision to have a LLC and not to make the Public Order Service a department of the municipal administrative organization rested partly on reasons of economy and flexibility. It was also a political compromise. The largest party in Linz, the SPÖ, wanted to prevent the Public Order Service from becoming a more repressive kind of organization, which might easily happen after a future political change of municipal government in Linz. By making the Public Order Service more autonomous, it was assumed that this risk would be smaller. The compromise was a LLC (which was actually against the wishes of the ÖVP).

There was also another compromise. The social democrats in Linz did not want the formal goals of the Public Order Service to be defined in terms of security (*Sicherheit*). The compromise was that initially the service's goals were defined in terms of cleanliness (*Sauberkeit)* and order *(Ordnung*). The objectives of the Linz Public Order Service are defined as *'to enforce order and cleanliness and to reduce wrongs and dangers.'*[39] It should also contribute to citizens' feelings of security. With this formulation, given the Austrian context and the prevailing views there, the suggestion could be avoided that the Public Order Service of Linz would still be (or become) a 'kind of police organization'.[40]

The specific tasks of the Linz Public Order Service are defined as: providing services to citizens (including the provision of information); reporting dangers to the municipal government, police or fire brigade; preventing crime; assisting the victims of crime; notifying illegally dumped waste or garbage; surveillance in regard to the prohibition of dogs without a leash; control of certain rules relating to 'youth protection' (*Jugendschutz)* (including bans on persons under the age of

36 Interview with respondent 5 Austria; E. Watzl, *Start Stadtwache*, Linz, 31 August 2010, http://linzstadt.oevp.at/uploads/media/PK_Start_Stadtwache.pdf, retrieved 13 September 2012; S. Mayr, *Juhu, Linz wird endlich sicher!*, 7 December 2009, http://severinmayr.at/2009/12/juhu-linz-wird-endlich-sicher/, retrieved 13 September 2012; Sozialistsiche Jugend Linz, *Stadt Linz braucht keine Ersatz-sheriffs*, 7 December 2008, www.sj-linz.at/news,1,28,26,75,__ankuendigung_medienaktion_stadtwache,news-detail.php, retrieved at 23 November 2012.

37 In German: GmbH.

38 Unless otherwise noted, information in this section is based on interview with respondent 5 Austria.

39 *Errichtungserklärung Ordnungsdienst Linz*, Linz, 2010.

40 E. Watzl, *Start Stadtwache*, Linz, August 31st 2010, http://linzstadt.oevp.at/uploads/media/PK_Start_Stadtwache.pdf, retrieved 13 September 2012.

fourteen from smoking, drinking alcoholic beverages, and being alone on the streets at night); surveillance of illegal street music; actions against illegal beggars; the enforcement of certain local regulations (such as those relating to camping along the River Danube) and, if necessary, submitting reports.[41]

For most of its tasks, the Linz Public Order Service has no special powers beyond the Everyman's right. In contrast to Styria, the province of Upper Austria (*Oberösterreich*) does not have an (amended) Surveillance Agency Act (*Aufsichtsorgangesetz)* as a legal basis for such powers.

The only exception here is that the Linz Public Order Service has the power to enforce rules against what is called 'aggressive or organized' forms of begging. This power is based on an appendix to the provincial Police Penal Law (*Polizeistrafgesetz*) of Upper Austria. The public order guards of the Linz Public Order Service are entitled to use coercion to hold an 'aggressive' beggar and hand him over to the police. The Linz public order guards are also entitled to confiscate the proceeds of begging and impose an administrative fine up to a maximum of € 2,200.[42]

The Linz Public Order Service has 30 public order guards. Their main task is foot patrol in pairs, if necessary by public transport, between 8:00 and 24:00 hrs.[43] These foot patrols are performed throughout the city, with the centre and some other sites getting extra attention.

During their patrols the public order guards of the Linz Public Order Service wear a recognizable uniform (red t-shirt, sweater or jacket with black trousers). In Linz it was decided that the uniform of these public order guards should not be similar to that of the police. In order to avoid any suggestion that these public order guards are 'police', they have no weapons, pepper spray or handcuffs. They only have a mobile phone, a pocket torch and a camera. The camera can be used to take pictures of illegal garbage dumping as evidence.

Initially the police in Linz were opposed to the introduction of a municipal Public Order Service. Police officers feared that the presence of the public order guards would result in many clashes and conflicts with citizens and this would mean a higher workload for the police. The police attitude has changed since then. At least at the level of the 'management cops' (Reuss-Ianni, 1983), the police now support the existence of the Linz municipal Public Order Service. The main reason for this change of attitude is probably that the police have noticed that it has not resulted in more work for them, but, on the contrary, the police have been able to offload some activities that the officers do not regard as very attractive.

41 *Errichtungserklärung Ordnungsdienst Linz*, Linz, 2010.

42 E. Watzl, *Start Stadtwache*, Linz, August the 31th of 2010, http://linz-stadt.oevp.at/uploads/media/PK_Start_Stadtwache.pdf, retrieved 13 September 2012.

43 The Public Order Service Linz does not have cars at its disposal., which means that the power to hold 'aggressive beggars' is not widely used. Municipal guards would have to take 'aggressive beggars' on foot to the next police station, which is not a very practical and encouraging situation to undergo frequently.

The general feeling in the Linz Public Order Service is that the establishment of their organization has given the police an excuse to withdraw even further from daily patrol and the local policing of social disorder and petty crime, and that it has contributed to a decreased visible presence in the public space. In practice, cooperation with the police in Linz seems to be rather poor. Information is exchanged only irregularly; police officers and public order guards only have rare contacts.

The local political debate has persisted ever since the proposal was made for a Public Order Service In Linz. Especially the Green Party and the citizen initiative 'Linz needs no public order guards' (*'Linz braucht keine Stadtwache')* continue to oppose the service and its work.[44] For example, the ban on aggressive begging has been criticized as an attempt to criminalize the very poor. The critical Platform Community Guards Linz (*Plattform Stadtwache Linz)* has calculated that the costs of the Public Order Service are much higher than the contribution it makes to public safety. The Linz Green Party called for abolition of the Public Order Service,[45] but their motion submitted to the Linz municipal council (September 2011) did not gain sufficient political support.[46] The critical Platform decided to set up a hotline where citizens could complain about incidents with the public order guards of the Public Order Service.[47]

On the opposite wing of Linz local politics, the conservative Austrian People's Party (ÖVP) and in particular the far-right Free Party of Austria (FPÖ) are seeking to expand the powers of the municipal Public Order Service. Even as early as the start of 2009, the FPÖ wanted the public order guards to be equipped with baton and pepper spray.[48] In 2011 the FPÖ and the ÖVP repeated their request for pepper spray.[49] In 2012, there was a political debate in Linz about the question of whether the public order guards should have more powers to determine the identities of persons who systematically break the rules regarding dogs being on a lead.

---

44 Inter alia www.stadtwachelinz.at and www.nachrichten.at/oberoesterreich/linz/art66,699318, retrieved 13 September 2012.

45 OÖNachrichten, Nachrichten.at, *Grüne wollen Linzer Stadtwache auflösen*, 30 August 2011, www.nachrichten.at/oberoesterreich/linz/art66,699318, retrieved 13 September 2012.

46 Beilage zum Amtsblatt der Landeshauptstad Linz Folge 7/2011 Protokoll über die 18. Sitzung des Gemeinderates der Landeshauptstadt Linz am Donnerstag, 15. September 2011, www.linz.at/Politik/GrSitzungen/doc/18999113622_18_Sitzung_15_09_11.pdf, retrieved 26 November 2012.

47 www.stadtwachelinz.at/meldestelle, retrieved 26 November 2012.

48 www.pichlingpartei.at/wbb3/index.php?page=Thread&postID=177, retrieved 23 November 2012.

49 OÖNachrichten. Nachrichten.at, *Pfefferspray für Linzer Stadtwache? Schwarz-Blau kontra Rot-Grün*, 19 May 2011, www.nachrichten.at/oberoesterreich/linz/art66,626204, retrieved 13 September 2012.

4.4 Private security in the public space

Private security in Austria

About 11,000 persons were employed in the private security industry in Austria in 2010, with about 200 companies operating in the sector. As in many other countries, the market in Austria is dominated by a few large companies (CoESS, 2011).[50] Private security in Austria has grown strongly over the past fifteen years (Fuchs, 2005: 21; CoESS, 2011). Available data indicate, however, that the private security industry in Austria is still relatively modest in comparison with other European countries, both in relation to the Austrian population and the number of police officers. In terms of size, the Austrian private security industry had the third lowest ranking of fifteen European countries in the mid-1990s (Hemmer & Bauer, 2003; Button, 2007), a result that was recently confirmed by Fuchs (2012).

Austria has no special legislation for the regulation of private security. However, four other elements are important here. First, the Everyman's right also applies to private security officers in Austria. On the basis of the Austrian Criminal Code (*Strafgesetzbuch*) and the Code of Criminal Procedure (*Strafprozessordnung*), Everyman's right means that private security officers, just like any citizen in the country, have rights such as self defence/emergency assistance (*Notwehr/Nothilfe*) and the right to 'report and arrest' (Fuchs, 2005: 149-192). Private security officers, working in a non-public territory that is private property, may have 'house right' (*Hausrecht*). The qualification 'non-public' is necessary here, because in Austria the public nature of a territory does not depend on its ownership, but on the question of whether the area is apparently accessible to the general public. A private security officer, working in a large privately owned shopping mall, does not have 'house right' (Fuchs, 2005: 21-41 and 93-97).[51]
Secondly, insofar as there is a regulation of private security in Austria, its legal basis lies in the Trade and Industry Act (*Gewerbeordnung*).[52] The general aim of the Act is to regulate the broad domains of industry, private security and businesses. Private security (both private investigation and private security guards) is one of the sectors that is distinguished in the Act. The Act contains of rules and regulations for private security, such as: the uniforms of private security officers; licensing requirements for a private security company; permission to run such a company; some requirements with which employees and employers in

50 Ruhe und Ordnung – Das Sicherheitsmagazin, *Dritter Sicherheitssektor hat in Österreich 16.000 Mitarbeiter*, 10 September 2010, http://sicherheitswien.wordpress.com/2010/09/24/dritter-sicherheitssektor-hat-in-oeste, retrieved 22 October 2012.

51 This might imply that the frequently cited thesis that the increasing role of private security in the urban semipublicspace (mass private property) (Shearing and Stenning, 1981; Jones and Newburn, 1999) results in social exclusion, would not apply to Austria.

52 *Gewerbeordnung*, Articles 129 and 130.

the private security industry must comply. Austria has no licensing system for private security employees. The requirements for employees and employers relate to their age, mastery of the German language and level of education, and there is a check on behaviour/criminal record. Persons employed by the police are not permitted to work in the private security sector. There is no set of clear quality standards for private security in Austria (Fuchs, 2005: 205-214; CoESS, 2011). As a result, one of the interviewees described the regulation of private security in Austria as 'weak'.[53]

Thirdly, in Austria there are no general regulations concerning the question of whether private security companies can be involved in government security tasks. Each policy domain has its own specific regulations, such as the control of airline passengers, parking rules, major events, tolls on highways, and the surveillance of (stationary and moving) traffic. The result is an opaque complex of rules and regulations (cf. Stolzlechner & Horvath, 2009).

Finally, Austria has no separate legislation for the possession of firearms by private security officers. The general rules and regulations of the Arms Act (*Waffengesetz)* apply. Any individual citizen in Austria is entitled to apply for a firearms licence. This also applies to individual private security officers, who must file the application on their own account (not that of the company). The inspectorate focuses on the question of whether the individual private security officer is eligible for a firearms licence. The mere fact that an officer is working in the security sector is not a sufficient motive for the granting of a licence. However, the licence may still be granted on grounds of specific hazards relating to work in the security sector (Fuchs, 2005: 214-215). For instance, such grounds may relate to security guards working in cash transport or the security of a bank building. As a result it is not unusual in Austria to see armed private security guards walking in the streets. In 2010 it was estimated that about 600 private security officers were allowed to carry weapons in Austria (CoESS, 2011: 11).

The result is that there is a striking contrast between private security officers and municipal guards of the Public Order Services. It is not only that the public order guards working at the municipal Public Order Services are unarmed, but also that great pains are taken to avoid any association of the public order guards with repression, armaments or the police.

Private security in the public space

Traditionally the private security industry in Austria operated mainly in private space. It focused, for example, on access control, guarding certain areas, and the security of buildings. However, for the past ten to fifteen years private security in Austria has increasingly acquired a visible role in semipublic and public space (Fuchs, 2005).

53 Interview with respondent 6 Austria.

First, for the last decade Austria has acquired new, large, partly covered shopping centres. The largest and best-known example is the *Shopping City Süd* in Vösendorf, located to the south of Vienna. This large mall beside the highway houses about 330 shops with mainly covered walkways, squares and inner courtyards. It is located on privately owned land. The mall is visited weekly by tens of thousands of consumers. The Shopping City Süd not only offers customers the opportunity to buy all sorts of goods, it is also a recreation and entertainment area, with cinemas, bars, restaurants and beauty and fitness centres.
As in many other countries, these mass private properties (Shearing and Stenning, 1983) are of increasing importance for the Austrian private security industry. Large numbers of private security officers work in the malls, not only undertaking security tasks in the strict sense (such as the prevention of crime and disorder and the enforcement of house rules), but also doing housekeeping, customer care and visitor services (cf. Wakefield, 2006). The large *Shopping City Süd* mall not only has a significant number of private security officers, there is also a police station (where police officers do their work in a privately owned space).

Secondly, an increasing number of municipal governments in Austria contract private security officers to work in the public space. This phenomenon can be encountered even more frequently than the municipal Public Order Services.[54] It is estimated that at least forty to fifty municipal governments have contracted private security officers to work in the public space. Especially medium-sized municipalities, such as Tulln, Mödling, Wiener-Neustadt, Korneuburg, Schwechat, Lavanttal and Wals-Siezenheim use this kind of contract. These municipalities do not have a municipal police force (*Gemeindewachkörper*), nor did these municipal governments opt for a Public Order Service (*Ordnungsdienst*), presumably because such a municipal department will often be too expensive and would result in a rather inflexible situation. The municipal governments' need to contract private security is broadly comparable to the need that the large cities like Graz and Linz try to meet with the establishment of a municipal Public Order Service. In both cases there is a need for more visible, uniformed surveillance and enforcement officers in the public space – a need that the police do not meet. Instead of creating a municipal Public Order Service, local governments try fill the gap with private security officers.
The tasks of these private security officers may differ between the municipalities. In some cases the core of their work consists of (preventive) surveillance in the public space. In other municipalities such private security officers are also involved in the enforcement of parking regulations, the enforcement of public order, surveillance in nightlife areas or at major events.[55] The terms used for these private officers may differ per municipality, such as Municipal Security

54 E-mail respondent 4 Austria, 11 September 2012.
55 E-mail of respondent 4 Austria, 6 September 2012.

Department (*Kommunale Sicherheitsdienst), City Guard* or *City Patrol*. These private security officers usually wear a uniform when they work in the public space, so the public can recognize them.
In some Austrian municipalities it seems that private security officers who are contracted by a local government are armed when they are on duty. The mass media report for instance that in the municipality of Tulln private security officers of the Skorpion company carry handcuffs, pepper spray and a pistol during their night patrols on behalf of the municipal government.[56] However, the formal powers of these private security officers are only those of the *Jedermannsrecht* (Everyman's right).

City Guards in Mödling

In Austria decisions to contract private security officers in the public space are made at the local level. To get a better view of this phenomenon, one example is analysed in more detail. The municipality of Mödling is located twenty kilometres south of Vienna. It is a small town of about 20,500 inhabitants and with an important role in the surrounding region.
In approximately 2004 and 2005 the first private security officers in the public space were deployed in Mödling. Employees of the security company *Securitas* started to patrol in the shopping streets in the old town. These *City Guards* were contracted by shopkeepers who also financed the scheme. The visible presence of City Guards in the centre of Mödling was intended to reduce theft and vandalism and enhance feelings of security, both of shopkeepers and customers. In addition, the City Guards were to escort customers who had purchased an expensive item from the store to their cars a combination of service and crime prevention.

In 2005, it turned out that the position of these private City Guards was not an uncontested issue. Representatives of the social-democratic party (SPÖ) in Mödling stated they were unhappy with the private security officers patrolling on behalf of shopkeepers. In their view security in the public space should primarily be the responsibility of the state. They demanded that the City Guards should not be armed under any circumstances. They also sought clarity about the City Guards' powers. The shopkeepers in Mödling defended themselves by arguing that the City Guards were never meant to be *'private sheriffs'* or *'private police'*. Although the City Guards were at that time not contracted by the local government and their involvement was not based on any political decision, the mayor of Mödling (a member of the Austrian People's Party, ÖVP) said that he looked

56 Die Zeit online 02.04.2009; comparable information in Die Zeit Online, 06.06.2012 about the municipality of Jedlersdorf. In the latter case the private security officers were contracted by a university.

favourably on this initiative and even that he could imagine arming these private security officers.[57]

A new situation arose in 2009,[58] when the local government of Mödling decided to contract several types of private security officer, once again employed by the private security company *Securitas*. This decision was taken under the local security management policy of the municipality of Mödling. Four traffic wardens and two so-called *Service Guards* were put under a more or less permanent contract. These Service Guards are quite similar to the previous City Guards, both in their goals and in their working methods. In addition, ten to fifteen times a year private security officers are contracted for surveillance tasks in the public space in Mödling, during one of the many public events that are annually organized there. The number of contracted private security officers varies from two to thirty per event. The length of their deployment can vary from one to seven days. Ninety per cent of the financial costs of contracting these private security officers is funded by the municipal government, the rest by an organization of local shopkeepers.

The municipal government of Mödling itself does not contract the private security company *Securitas*. The municipal government has delegated a significant part of its operational activities to a privatized company: *City Management,* the shares of which are wholly owned by the municipal government. The main argument of the Mödling local government in favour of this quasi-privatization is that it should create a certain distance between municipal operational activities and local (party) politics. The private security officers of Securitas are contracted by the quasi-private company *City Management*.

To understand security in the public space in Mödling, the *Service Guards* are most relevant. The main task of these private guards is surveillance by patrolling the shopping streets of the old town, especially some notorious hotspots. They have to talk to beggars, drunks, and members of juvenile groups hanging around, including addressing their behaviour that could cause nuisance and feelings of insecurity to the citizens of Mödling, and asking them either to change their behaviour or remove themselves. If necessary the Service Guards should call the police. The visible presence of the private Service Guards should promote feelings of security and reassure customers.

The Service Guards have no special powers. Often they do not even wear uniforms when on duty. They have no firearms. It is quite remarkable that representatives of the local police and of the municipal *City Management*, when asked, did not know whether the Service Guards carried pepper spray, batons or handcuffs

57 ORF.at, *Privater Sicherheitsdienst in Innenstadt*, 17 July 2005, http://noev1.orf.at/stories/46052; Wien-heute.at, *Privater Sicherheitsdienst soll Kaufleute und Kunden schützen*, www.wien-heute.at/p-8475.php?subakt=newcom both retrieved 11 September 2012.

58 Interviews with respondents 1 and 2 Austria.

during their patrol. However, when asked they said they could not rule this out; in their view that was the responsibility of the private security company.

There is only a modest degree of cooperation between the police and the Service Guards in Módling. Information is hardly exchanged. The police do not have operational control over the Service Guards and there are no joint briefings. If any information is exchanged, that happens informally, for example when Service Guards and police officers meet by chance during their street patrols. One factor that contributes to the distance between the police and the Service Guards (in Mödling and elsewhere) is that the police do not consider the enforcement of local administrative regulations (*Ortspolizeilicher Verordnungen*) to be their proper task, but as a responsibility of the municipal government only.

In principle the municipal government of Mödling might be able to create its own municipal police force (*Gemeindewachkörper*) or a municipal Public Order Service. However, the municipal government decided to contract private security officers to patrol the public space in the old town centre. Managerial arguments were decisive here: contracting private security officers is cheaper, creates more flexibility and does not require the creation of a new municipal organization (which would be too large for the needs of this municipality).

4.5 Relations with the police

This chapter has already paid a lot of attention to the position of the police in Austria and the relations between the police and the public wardens and private guards. Some other issues are briefly discussed below.

The interviews suggest that since 2002 the police have gradually withdrawn from the local level and local priorities. The police reform of 2005 contributed to this process. In Austria a fundamental distinction is made between (regular) police work and the enforcement of local administrative regulations. Apart from the legal and practical sustainability of this distinction, this dogma encourages the Federal Police to often maintain a certain distance from local priorities and local issues of social disorder.

Although the police initially often voiced reservation about the introduction of Public Order Services, the interviews suggest that their original resistance has now largely disappeared. Nowadays, the presence of municipal wardens and guards seems increasingly to be used by the police as an argument to withdraw even further from local policing matters. Some interviewees think that these wardens and guards may provide an excuse for the police to neglect local issues of social disorder.

In practice, cooperation between the police and the municipal wardens and guards often seems to be quite poor in Austria. There is barely any steering by the police and virtually no exchange of information. The police often say that they are short of time and other resources to do this. Moreover, legal arguments are used by the police, such as the need to protect police information and the dogma of the fundamental difference between the domain of police work and the enforcement of local administrative regulations. However, two of the interviewees have a different view on the underlying motives of the police: they suggest that police officers often feel that local matters of social disorder are not sufficiently interesting. Moreover, the police often are said to look down on the municipal wardens and feel contempt for their work.

4.6 Conclusions

The development of plural policing in Austria depends closely on the specific national legal and institutional context. The predominant culture of governance, policy and police in Austria places relatively great emphasis on legalistic, formal and hierarchical elements. This specific context results in rather complex relations between the police forces, municipal wardens/guards and private security officers in the public space. Table 4.1 reviews these relations.

Table 4.1 Police forces, municipal wardens/guards and private security officers in the public space in Austria[59]

	Municipalities without Provincial Police Directorate	Cities with Provincial Police Directorate (big cities, *Statutarstädte*)	Other (especially) medium-sized municipalities contracting private security companies
– Federal police *(n = 1)*	X	X	X
– Municipal police *(n = 37)*	X		
– Public Order Service *(n = 10 to 15, estimated)*		X	
– The contracting of private security officers in public space *(n = 40 to 45, estimated)*			X

Despite this specific legal and institutional context, processes of plural policing are very similar to those in other countries. For the past decade or so the police have been withdrawing from local problems of social order and local priorities. Partly in response to this development, in Austria too there has been an increase

59 This table only represents empirical relations. In theory it might be possible to have combinations of municipal police and Public Order Service (only in cities without Provincial Police Directorate), of municipal police and private security officers in the public space, and of Public Order Service and private security officers. In practice however, these combinations cannot be found (for reasons described in this chapter).

in public wardens and private guards, playing an ever more prominent role in the public space.

To understand plural policing in Austria the dominant views on the police in this country are highly relevant. Police work is often defined in terms of the use of coercive means. Local issues, such as visible, uniformed surveillance in the streets, the maintenance of peace and social order, and service to citizens, increasingly seem not to be regarded as proper police work. This study has not attempted to determine the extent to which this view of police work corresponds with the police work as it is actually carried out on the streets, whether now or in the past.

Policing and security seem to be peculiarly politicized in Austria. Political differences about police and security have a remarkable impact. Existing views on police and security often reflect the traditional – and considerable – differences of opinion between the political right wing and the left. This is probably in line with the profound party political divisions in Austria, which for the past few decades have had a major impact in many social and political areas. The public debate in Austria has been especially relevant to the question of whether there should be any room for non-police wardens and patrol officers in the public space (cf. Fuchs, 2005). Much less attention is paid, for example, to questions concerning the conditions that surveillance and enforcement in public space should meet to guarantee the legal protection of citizens' rights. In this context the lack of (political) interest in complaints procedures is quite telling. None of the three municipalities analysed here (Graz, Linz and Mödling) has a specific complaint procedure. Citizens who wish to express their displeasure about decisions made by the municipal wardens or about how they have been treated, have to use the general procedures of the local administration. In one of these municipalities citizens should contact the Civil Service or Civil Affairs departments of the municipality if they want to complain.[60]

Finally, and in seeming contrast to the dominating legalistic culture in Austria, the regulation of these new forms of non-police policing is fairly poor in many respects. For instance, there is little certainty about the powers and tasks of Public Order Services. There is only a rudimentary specific legal basis for the regulation of private security. As a consequence, despite the predominant and traditional emphasis in Austria on the monopoly of the (central) state in policing and security, private security officers can be armed during their work on the streets.

60 Interview with respondent 2 Austria.

5 Belgium

The federal state of Belgium (about 11 million residents) consists of three language related regions: the Flemish region (where most people speak Dutch), the Walloon region (with most people speaking French) and the Brussels-Capital region. Next to these regions Belgium has three language communities: the Flemish community, the French community and the German-speaking community. Regions and communities have overlapping boundaries, but the territory of the German-speaking community lies wholly within the Walloon Region. Each region-community has its own government and parliament. Since the 1990s Belgium comprises 589 municipalities, which play an important role in public safety policy.

This chapter has a comparable structure to that of the other national chapters in this book. First a brief description is given of the police system in Belgium (5.1). Next, some important elements of national policy are dealt with (5.2), followed by a section on the local implementation of these policies (5.3). Then the role of private security in the public domain in Belgium is briefly discussed (5.4). Finally, the chapter deals with relationships between the non-police providers of policing and the police (5.5), the protection of citizens' rights (5.6), and some issues in the Belgian public debate on plural policing (5.7).

5.1 Police system

The police in Belgium underwent radical reform in 1998. A fragmented system of different police services (municipal police, judicial police and gendarmerie) was replaced by an 'integrated' police, consisting of one federal police force and 196 local (or '*zonal*') police forces.[1] The main reason for this reform was the lack of effectiveness of the old fragmented police system. The police came under severe criticism, which culminated in the well-known Dutroux case in 1996, when the police were accused of serious miscarriages.

1 'Wet van 07 december 1998 tot organisatie van een geïntegreerde politiedienst, gestructureerd op twee niveaus'. In: *Het Belgisch Staatsblad*, 5 January 1999.

The system of 'integrated' police consists of two levels, federal and local. The police forces at both levels have to cooperate and assist each other in the performance of their duties. Together the federal force and the zonal forces have to ensure 'integrated policing'. Whereas the zonal forces are responsible for the regular police work at the local level, the federal force concentrates on specialized and supralocal matters, and offers support services to the local police. According to the enacting legislation, the principle of an integrated police force should guarantee equivalent services throughout the country.
Since 2001 the police in Belgium have been obliged to work according to the principles of community-oriented policing (*'gemeenschapsgerichte politie'*). A Ministerial Circular gives the following interpretation of this term: the police should have a broad approach to problems of public safety and quality of life, the police should be closely integrated in society, should be visible to and approachable by citizens, and cooperate with communities to create solutions to local problems of public safety.[2] One of the measures behind the implementation of this model is that there must be one community police officer per 4,000 residents.[3]
This police reform was evaluated a decade later. One of the conclusions was that most of the zonal forces engaged in community policing, but that in practice it still caused some distress. There were too few community officers and the quality of community policing did not meet the required standards. Another relevant finding was that in practice police work often has to be supplemented by non-police providers of police services (Bruggeman et al., 2010: 60 and 85).

5.2 Community guards and community guard-recorders

Belgium has two categories of public non-police providers of policing in the public space. The first category consists of community guards (in Dutch *'gemeenschapswachten'* and in French *'guardiens de la paix'*) whose main task is patrol and surveillance, but who have no special powers at their disposal. Secondly there are, with an impossible and unpronounceable name, community guard-recorders (the literal translation of the rather complex expression *'gemeenschapswachten-vaststellers' or 'guardiens de la paix-constateurs'*). This latter category consists of enforcement officers, who are entitled to record certain offences in a so-called administrative report (*'bestuurlijk verslag')* (Devroe, 2012: 317).[4] This administrative report must be sent to an officer at the municipal

2 'Ministeriële omzendbrief CP1 van 27 mei 2003 betreffende Community Policing, definitie van de Belgische interpretatie van toepassing op de geïntegreerde politiedienst, gestructureerd op twee niveaus', In: *Het Belgisch Staatsblad*, 9 July 2003.

3 Article 2 of the Royal Decree 'K.B. van 17 september 2001 tot vaststelling van de organisatie- en werkingsnormen van de lokale politie etc.'. In: *Het Belgisch Staatsblad*,,12 October 2001.

4 This administrative report contains a description of the established infringement. If relevant, photographs of the situation can be included.

administration (called the sanctioning officer), who is entitled to apply a sanction (a fine) or to propose mediation (often community service).[5] The municipal Service of Community Guards employs both community guards and community guard-recorders.[6]
In 2009 the number of community guards (including community guard-recorders) in Belgium was estimated as 3,300 (ibid.: 338). About three per cent of these are community guard-recorders.[7] No more recent figures could be found.

Backgrounds

In the 1980s and 1990s several crisis situations and disasters in Belgium (like the Gang of Nivelles, the Heysel Stadium disaster and the Dutroux case) contributed to a sharp decline in the citizens' confidence in governmental institutions. The police and criminal justice agencies were fiercely criticized as a result.
In the 1990s public polls in Belgium showed that many citizens felt insecure in their own neighbourhoods and that these feelings of insecurity were often closely associated with social disorder. Higher levels of sensitivity, a loss of informal social control, and changes in the population resulting from immigration meant that petty forms of crime and disorder started to have a powerful impact on the quality of life. Many citizens lost confidence in the police and criminal justice agencies.
However, the public prosecution agency asserted with increasing frequency that given the high number of petty crimes, it did not have adequate resources. For that reason the Belgian government decided that responsibilities should be devolved to the local authorities. The result was that municipal governments gained more powers to settle these cases (Devroe, 2012: 369). This was achieved in 1999 with the Municipal Administrative Sanctions Act (MAS-Act).[8] The MAS-Act was an attempt to provide municipal authorities with more means to manage petty crime and social disorder.
The MAS-Act was mainly an initiative of the social democrats in the Flemish part of the country, especially the then Minister of the Interior, Louis Tobback, together with socialist mayors. The rise of the *Vlaams Blok* (a far-right nationalist political party) meant that public safety became a significant political issue. The socialist politicians felt they had to act decisively to steal a march on the *Vlaams*

5 Articles 119bis and 199ter of the New Municipal Act (In Dutch: 'Nieuwe Gemeentewet'). For minors a proposal for mediation is required.

6 Circular 'Ministeriële omzendbrief PREV 32' (2010). In: *Het Belgisch Staatsblad*, 3 May 2010.

7 Interview with respondent 3 Belgium. The small percentage of enforcement officers might be a consequence of the fact there are (almost) no community guard-recorders in Wallonia. The percentage in Flanders is presumably much greater.

8 In Dutch: '*Gemeentelijke Administratieve Sancties*' (GAS). 'Wet van 13 mei 1999 tot de invoering van de gemeentelijke administratieve sancties'. In: *Het Belgisch Staatsblad*, 10 June 1999.

Blok (ibid.: 363). The MAS-Act provided them with the means to pursue such a strategy.

The MAS-Act was a policy decision that was not based on an explicit theoretical model; pragmatic considerations were far more important. According to Devroe (2012, 357-386) the introduction of the municipal administrative sanctions had four main objectives.

- First, it should compensate for the enforcement deficit. At the local level it should contribute to an 'armed government'. The assumption was that the public prosecution agency should concentrate on the more serious forms of crime. The courts were said to be unable to handle many minor cases due to their heavy workload. Since the public prosecutor invariably dismissed petty cases, the credibility of the police and criminal justice agencies was eroded.
- It should meet the need of local governments to have means for their own enforcement strategies in relation to disorder and quality-of-life issues. This was to be seen as an integral element of municipal holistic public safety policies. MAS sanctions were seen as the repressive elements that could make 'soft' preventive strategies more effective.
- The use of MAS sanctions was presented as the final piece in a preventive policy.
- The MAS Act should also contribute to the need for an increasing level of control by making uniformed surveillance more visible, and should provide for the possibility of imposing sanctions if disorderly behaviour could not be changed in another way.

After the elections of 1999 Belgium got its first 'purple' government ('red' socialists and 'blue' liberals). Liberals headed the ministries whose tasks related to public safety. Public safety had a high priority for the liberal party. It was in those years that the notion of an integrated public safety policy became more important in Belgium.[9] The MAS Act was seen as an important instrument in this local policy. However, this MAS Act soon proved to have several serious shortcomings. One consequence was that for a long time it was unclear how and by whom the MAS Act could be applied in practice.[10] One of the interviewees suggested that these shortcomings arose because at that time there was more interest in Belgian police reform than in municipal administrative sanctions.[11] As a result the MAS Act was frequently amended in the following years.

9 Interview with respondent 1 Belgium.

10 One of the main shortcomings of the MAS Act 1999 was that only the police had the power to record an infringement, but these administrative sanctions had a very low priority for the police. See Devroe (2012), Chapter 7.

11 Interview with respondent 3 Belgium.

A specific element relates to the position of mayors in Belgium. Mayoral elections are held every six years. One of the mayor's main responsibilities has to do with public safety. Many mayors feel the pressure to meet the public's demands, especially in this policy domain. This could mean that the mayor might be unwilling to apply rules and procedures stemming from the national level, if he/she knew that this would not increase his/her chances at the elections. This is one factor that may have contributed to the gap between policies at the federal and the local level.[12]

After the police reform of the late 1990s the municipal police ceased to exist. On the one hand this implied that the mayor no longer had his own police force.[13] On the other hand, however, the overloaded public prosecutions agency said that it did not have the resources to process cases of petty crime and social disorder. Although there was now a MAS Act, the mayor still did not have the means to implement this system of administrative sanctions. In the late 1990s, however, in the context of various employment programmes and the call for more public safety, the federal government entered into contracts with local authorities that established budgets to permit the introduction of a multitude of *'new occupations in security'* (Enhus et al., 2005).[14] Most of these occupations were intended to comprise surveillance in the public space.[15]

These new wardens and guards gave rise to a great deal of confusion among citizens because of the many styles of uniforms they were wearing. The officers had no formal powers: they could only play a preventive role by addressing citizens and asking them to change their behaviour.

It was not until 2007 that this situation changed. The Community Guards Act (2007)[16] transformed many of these *'new occupations in security'* into one new category of wardens called the community guard. These new officers were to wear the same purple uniform in all Belgian municipalities, which, it was assumed, would reduce the public's confusion. Until that point the MAS Act could not be effectively used and the mayor had no potential means of controlling social disorder and petty crime. It was therefore decided to use the community guards to do just this: they were available, they were trained, and they were screened.

A similar argument led to the creation of the new position of community guard-recorder in the Act of 2007. Compared to the community guard, these community guard-recorders were also given the formal authority to report certain forms

12 Interviews with respondents 2 and 3 Belgium.

13 Interview with respondent 3 Belgium.

14 Some examples of these new *'new positions in security'*: neighbourhood father, neighbourhood supervisor, bicycle parking guard, coach entertainment areas, city guard, migrants city guard, playground supervisor and nuisance prevention worker.

15 Interview with respondent 3 Belgium.

16 'Wet van 15 mei 2007 tot instelling van de functie van gemeenschapswacht, tot instelling van de dienst gemeenschapswachten en tot wijziging van artikel 119bis van de nieuwe gemeentewet'. In: *Het Belgisch Staatsblad*, 29 June 2007.

of social disorder or anti-social behaviour. Their reports could provide the basis for an administrative sanction.[17] This legal decision at last supplemented the MAS Act with an instrument for its effective implementation (Devroe, 2012: 338). The community guard-recorder does not impose the administrative sanction. He or she sends the report to the municipal 'sanctioning officer' and it is the sanctioning officer who decides on subsequent action: drop the matter, impose an administrative sanction, or mediation.[18] This dual system, with a split between the official who records an infringement and the official who decides on the sanction, is given legitimacy by the constitutional argument of a separation of powers.[19]

The MAS Act distinguishes between two categories of 'infringement'.[20] The first category consists of 'strictly municipal infringements' (eigen inbreuken, literally translated: 'own infringements'): these are disruptions to what is called cleanliness, health, safety and public peace, including social order. These are matters that can be dealt with only by means of an administrative sanction.
The second category, called 'mixed infringements', are an element of criminal law, but may be settled by a local government by means of an administrative sanction. These more serious infringements include damage or destruction of property, vandalism, nighttime noise, insult, threat, intentional injury and certain forms of theft.
MAS violations can be reported by different categories of officers: police, community guard-recorders, officers of public transport companies and, under certain circumstances, private security guards. However, these various professional groups are not authorized to report every kind of infringement: a distinction is made between 'petty' and 'severe mixed' infringements. Community guard-recorders are only authorized to record violations that are included in the 'strictly municipal infringements' category. Reports of 'severe mixed infringements' can only be drawn up by the police.

If a violation falls under the 'strictly municipal infringements' category, the administrative report drawn up by the community guard-recorder is sent to the municipal sanctioning officer, who is authorized to impose a MAS sanction (such as a fine). In the case of a 'light mixed infringement' the administrative report is sent to the public prosecution agency. The municipal sanctioning officer is only permitted to take action if the public prosecutor has not decided to prosecute within a period of two months. From that moment, the sanctioning officer is authorized to impose a MAS sanction. In the case of a 'severe mixed infringement' the municipal sanctioning officer is only permitted to impose a MAS sanc-

17 Interview with respondent 3 Belgium.
18 As previously mentioned: for minor offenders a proposal for mediation is mandatory.
19 Interview with respondent 3 Belgium.
20 Based on Cops, Put and Pleysier (2012) and De Belser (2012).

tion if the public prosecutor has explicitly decided not to prosecute and if in his/her view an administrative sanction is appropriate.

Tasks and powers

According to the Community Guards Act of 2007 community guards and community guard-recorders are required to promote citizens' feelings of security, and prevent public disorder and crime. The officers should meet these objectives through a range of activities, such as informing citizens about problems of public safety, making the general public more aware of security and crime prevention, informing car drivers about risks and the regulation of traffic safety, assisting children, elderly and disabled persons to cross the road, and keeping watch over persons in large-scale events. Only the community guard-recorders are also authorized to record infringements of municipal regulations and ordinances, which may be the basis for the imposition of a MAS sanction.
Both community guards and community guard-recorders are only allowed to work in the public space (public roads and other freely accessible places) in the territory of the municipality. They are not permitted to work in private spaces, even if these spaces are open to the general public (e.g. malls).[21]

According to the Community Guards Act (2007), community guards and community guard-recorders are required to interact with the citizenry in '*courteous dialogue*'. This implies that the officers may request a citizen to modify his behaviour and respect the rules.[22]
In Belgium community guards dispose only of the powers that are also at the disposal of any citizen. They are authorized to hold a person caught in the act while waiting for the police. Every Belgian citizen is authorized to take such action.
The community guard-recorders' main formal power is that they can record a violation of municipal regulations and ordinances that are included in the category of 'strictly municipal infringements'.[23] They are also entitled to request the offender to produce identity documents. However, if the person refuses to provide this information, the use of coercion is not permitted.[24]
In the public debate on the powers of community guard-recorders there is a strong contrast between Flanders and Wallonia. In Wallonia there are almost no community guard-recorders, only community guards ('*guardien de la paix*'). In Flanders, by contrast, the use of community guard-recorders is widespread and

21 The 4th Article of the Community Guards Act (2007); and the Circular 'Ministeriële omzendbrief PREV 32' (2010).
22 The 14th Article of the Community Guards Act (2007); and the Circular 'Ministeriële omzendbrief PREV 32' (2010).
23 Article 119bis, § 6 of the *Nieuwe Gemeentewet* (New Municipal Act).
24 Circular 'Ministeriële omzendbrief PREV 32 etc.' (2010).

there is even fairly strong pressure to give these municipal officers more formal powers.
At the time this study was carried out, the general expectation was that the formal powers of community guard-recorders would be expanded in the near future. Certain police tasks may be transferred to the community guard-recorders. Joint patrol with the police might also be permitted. One of the interviewees expected that in the near future community guards and community guard-recorders would not be restricted to municipal territory, but to the (usually larger) territory of the police zone. He also expected that the work of these municipal officers would increasingly come to form an integral part of regular police work. As a consequence, the community guard-recorders might become more police-like and lose their own specific character as representatives of the municipal administration.[25]
Several interviewees also expected the numbers of community guards and community guard-recorders to increase, despite the current era of austerity. The main reason for this is that the future community guard-recorders would probably plug the gaps left by the police, who do not pay sufficient attention to local problems of social disorder (cf. Smeets, 2008: 190).[26]

Quality standards, equipment and uniform

Municipal community guards and community guard-recorders have to meet the following standards: they must be at least eighteen years of age, have no record of convictions, or any other transgression that may lower their trustworthiness. The officers are not allowed to operate simultaneously as a private security guard, private investigator, or to be employed by the police. They must have undergone suitable, recognized training, which should include subjects such as their rights and duties, verbal and non-verbal communication, conflict management, and first aid.[27]
Community guards must also be a resident of an EU member state. The additional requirements for community guard-recorders are somewhat stricter: they must have Belgian nationality; they must have a certificate of higher secondary education, or else a certificate of lower secondary education combined with at least five years' work experience with the municipal administration; they must have received training in municipal administrative sanctions, provided by an accredited organization; finally, both community guards and community guard-recorders should have *'respect for fellow human beings, civic spirit, a resilience regarding aggressive behaviour, self control and respect for duty and procedure'*.[28]

25 Interview with respondent 3 Belgium.
26 Also interview with respondent 4 Belgium.
27 Article 10 of the Community Guards Act (2007).
28 Article 8 of the Community Guards Act (2007); and the Circular 'Ministeriële omzendbrief PREV 32' (2010).

One of the interviewees assumes that in the future the domain of the community guards will be subject to ongoing specialization. In combination with the expected extension of their formal powers, the quality requirements for community guard-recorders will probably be too low. He expects several serious problems if the standards are raised. Many of the present community guards and community guard-recorders are not well educated and were long-term unemployed before they were appointed to the job. It has proved difficult to give them more training. A significant point is that they currently must receive training, but do not have to pass an exam. If the standards were to be raised and applied more strictly, many of the present guards would probably have to be fired, which is viewed as unacceptable.[29]

Community guards and community guard-recorders must be recognizable to the general public. They have to wear a purple uniform with a standard, recognizable insignia or emblem on it. The law states they are not allowed to work in civilian clothes. Their identification card must be visible to citizens. Moreover, there has to be a clear and visible distinction between community guards and community guard-recorders. The latter officers have to wear an armband with the term *'Vaststeller'* (Recorder) on the right sleeve of their uniform. They carry no weapons, handcuffs or pepper spray.[30]

5.3 Differences in local implementation

The local implementation of community guards and community guard-recorders varies a great deal. Belgian municipal authorities have wide discretion to establish their own local public safety policies and may modify federal policies according to their own local context. One of the interviewees, working at the federal level, said it is something of an illusion to think that there is one uniform Belgian implementation style.[31]

Just a small, but striking example is that not all municipal governments comply with the legal requirement that community guards and community guard-recorders have to wear a purple uniform. In some cases they wear civilian clothes, in others they have uniforms in other styles and colours. Local preferences and budgetary reasons mean that local authorities prefer their own individual uniforms. In practice the federal government leaves things as they are.[32]

29 Interview with respondent 3 Belgium.

30 Article 11 and 13 of the Article of the Community Guards Act (2007); and the Circular 'Ministeriële omzendbrief PREV 32' (2010).

31 Interview with respondent 3 Belgium.

32 Interview with respondents 2 and 3 Belgium.

As already noted, community guards and community guard-recorders should not, formally speaking, be placed under the police. In some municipalities this still happens, however, with in some cases direct management of the guards by the police (Devroe, 2012: 411-412). One of the interviewees said it was *'an open secret'* that certain police chiefs use the community guards for regular police work. It is said to be difficult for the federal government to change this practice because the community guards and community guard-recorders are increasingly funded by the municipal authorities.[33]

As already noted, Wallonia has almost no community guard-recorders. To a significant degree the difference between the two regions in Belgium results from divergent views on public safety and crime prevention, and on the role of government in general. A more government-centred ideology dominates in Wallonia, with a general consensus that policing should be done by the police.[34]

To gain a better view of the diversity of local practices among community guards and community guard-recorders, we look at four municipalities in Belgium, two in Flanders (Antwerp and Ghent), one in Wallonia (Liège), and one in the Brussels region.

Antwerp[35]

Local public safety policy in the city of Antwerp (506,000 inhabitants[36]) lays a strong emphasis on the integrated approach. The work of community guards and community guard-recorders should be understood in the context of the more general policy of the city department *Living Together* (*'Samenleven'*), which embraces both preventive and repressive strategies.

Community guards in Antwerp (also called neighbourhood supervisors) have mainly preventive tasks. They conduct visible patrols in the streets, perform surveillance in the public space, establish contacts with citizens in the neighbourhoods, write reports of observed overdue maintenance in the streets, make citizens aware of public rules and regulation, and mediate in conflicts. The general goal behind these activities is to promote the quality of life in the Antwerp neighbourhoods.

The city of Antwerp has eighteen fulltime and fifteen voluntary community guard-recorders. Members of the latter category are employed, for example, in the municipal cleaning service department. In addition to their regular work they are community guard-recorders in the evenings. The work of community guard-recorders is mainly repressive. Their activities are focused at specific

33 Interview with respondent 3 Belgium.

34 Interview with respondent 4 Belgium.

35 Unless otherwise stated, based upon interview with respondent 2 Belgium.

36 City of Antwerp, www.antwerpen.buurtmonitor.be, retrieved 10 December 2012.

moments and locations (hotspots), combating problems as illegal dumping, improper placement of garbage, graffiti and urinating in public. Community guard-recorders do not wear a uniform during their shift, even though this is a legal requirement. They may still wear the armband with the word 'Recorder', and carry their identity card with them.

In the year 2011 the Antwerp community guard-recorders produced over 8,500 reports. These reports are processed by a unit consisting of five sanctioning officers and a support staff of 30 persons in the municipal department *Living Together*. This unit not only handles the reports of the community guard-recorders, but also the MAS charges drawn up by the police. In 2011, the police issued 13,000 MAS fines. This implies that in 2011 municipal officers and police officers produced a total of about 21,500 MAS reports. The cases are first screened by support staff of the municipal unit, ahead of a more or less individual decision by the sanctioning officer. In two-thirds of these cases the municipal sanctioning officers proposed mediation. In the remainder a MAS sanction (an administrative fine) was imposed.

The city of Antwerp considers one of the main advantages of the MAS system to be its potential to keep the police involved in the management of petty crime and disorder. In the past the police largely backed out of this task and the public prosecution agency denied its responsibility, hiding behind complaints of a huge workload. The city of Antwerp uses the MAS Act as a tool to compel the police to intensify their efforts. This strategy appears to have been successful, given the high number of MAS fines.

The city of Antwerp uses several strategies to keep the police involved. At different levels, agreements are made between the city, the police and community guard-recorders to coordinate the efforts of these three agencies. Common priorities are defined and joint campaigns are launched, concentrating on problems like the illegal dumping of garbage. In such cases the police and community guards frequently participate in joint patrols.

In Antwerp, community guards and community guard-recorders working on the streets have a direct line of communication with the police. They have a red button at their disposal in case they are confronted with danger. In addition, neighbourhood police officers and community guards and community guard-recorders often have regular informal relations and keep in touch using mobile phones.

Ghent[37]

The city of Ghent (247,000 inhabitants[38]) has had community guards since the early 1990s. Initially these jobs were created as additional employment for the

37 This section is based on the interviews with respondents 5 and 6 Belgium (unless otherwise indicated).

38 City of Ghent, www.gent.be/gentincijfers, retrieved 10 December 2012.

long-term unemployed. The city of Ghent defined the introduction of the community guards as mainly a preventive measure. The amendment of the MAS Act in 2007 created much more scope for MAS fines. However, in Ghent there was (and still is) fairly strong resistance to excessive repression in the management of disorder, certainly by comparison with Antwerp.

In 2012 the Service of Community Guards of the city of Ghent had three teams. First, a team of twenty community guards has preventive patrol as its main task. These community guards have no special powers. Secondly, there is a team of seventeen community guards who do surveillance work on Ghent public transport. Once again, they have no special powers, even in respect of fare dodgers. This task is reserved for employees of the public transport company itself. Thirdly, Ghent has a team of four community guard-recorders.[39] The reason that this team is so small reflects the fact that the focus in Ghent is primarily on prevention rather than repression. Finally, the city of Ghent has fifteen to twenty employees who are occasionally used as 'Chinese volunteers' (i.e. forced volunteers) as community guard-recorders.

With the exception of the guards working on public transport, the guards work mainly in the nineteenth-century area of Ghent, where problems of social disorder are concentrated.

In general the strategies adopted in Ghent resemble those elsewhere in Belgium. If community-guards observe problems like illegal dumping, they talk to the citizens about it and report the case to the appropriate authority for further disposition. Their main task is to make citizens aware of their problematic behaviour. The guards are also seen as the eyes and ears of the local authorities. Community guard-recorders can ask citizens to show their ID documents and then write a record. In Ghent the guard is explicitly asked also to mention mitigating circumstances in the administrative record. In contrast to the federal rules, in Ghent it is possible to appeal fines lower than € 62.50.

Between 2006 and 2009 the number of MAS reports in Ghent rose sharply from 1,296 to 3,494. In the first quarter of 2012 there was a further increase by almost a half. A main factor contributing to this growth is the establishment of a new 'social disorder' team under the Ghent police. However the number of MAS reports written in 2012 by municipal workers was still almost four times greater than those submitted by the police.[40] Both the total number of MAS reports, and the police force's contribution to it, are significantly lower in Ghent than in Antwerp. This is the case even after paying attention to the difference in population size between the two cities.

Nevertheless, in Ghent the dominant view is that prevention should be more important than repression. For instance, the community guards prefer not be

39 An extension of this team to 8.8 FTE is planned for the near future.

40 PowerPoint presentation *'Gemeentelijke Administratieve Sancties Evaluatievergadering GAS 2011'* (City of Ghent).

associated with the work of the community guard-recorders. They fear that the repressive image of community guard-recorders might adversely affect their own relations with citizens. That is the reason why they want their colleagues to wear a different uniform, so that citizens will see the difference. At the policy level, this strong focus on prevention means that the city of Ghent is generally unhappy with the proposed extension of MAS sanctions. It is believed that MAS should only deal with problems of disorder. In this view more serious forms of crime should not be handled by municipalities. The latter procedures demand stronger protection of citizens' rights and more legal safeguards. Moreover, there are fears in Ghent that MAS might also be used for such issues as a burka ban. The city of Ghent does not support the proposed lower age limit. In conclusion, the cities of Ghent and Antwerp differ strongly in their views on the MAS system.

In the past few years, Ghent has seen a considerable improvement in cooperation with the police in the implementation of the MAS Act. The social disorder team introduced under the Ghent police had a contributory role in this. Cooperation with the police takes the form of information exchange during special projects or at large events. There is no structural exchange of information, for example in the form of regular briefings. To a certain extent the police and municipal administration remain two separate worlds.

One of the main problems in Ghent has to do with the increasing numbers of MAS reports. These have to be handled by a single municipal sanctioning officer. Moreover, collecting fines is often not easy: the address of the suspect is often not easy to trace, the offender has moved abroad, or you cannot squeeze blood out of a stone.

Liège[41]

Since 1999 in the city of Liège (190,000 inhabitants[42]) the MAS Act has scarcely been applied, either by the municipal authorities or the police. The notion of an integrated, multi-agency approach in local security policy does not hold much sway there, in contrast to the city of Antwerp, for example. The local government generally focuses more on a traditional policy on poverty and the promotion of social cohesion, rather than a local, integrated public safety policy. In Liège the police are still seen as the central actor and coordinator of local security and policing.

In general, significantly less attention is paid in Liège to problems of social disorder. In contrast to Antwerp, for example, it looks as if citizens' complaints about social disorder are not taken as seriously as feelings of insecurity that require a strong, visible response by local authorities and agencies. The management of

41 Information on the situation in the City of Liège is based entirely on Devroe (2012: 393-470).

42 Website of the city of Liège: http://luik.be, retrieved 10 December 2012.

social disorder is still primarily defined as the task and responsibility of the police.

Contrary to what federal rules require, the community guards in Liège are based in police stations. The police force has fourteen stations, distributed throughout the city. The police organization is also seen as responsible for the governance of the community guards. The work performed by community guards is based on the principle that they are only permitted to perform surveillance tasks (such as patrols) and that they should not do (other types of) police work. The main argument for the strict division between the police and community guards is the fear that a wider range of tasks for the community guards might damage the public image of the police force and might undermine the public's recognition of the specific expertise of neighbourhood police officers.

That is also the main reason why the city of Liège has no community guard-recorders. In some cases, however, police officers and community guards participate in a joint patrol.

Because Liège has no community guard-recorders, almost no administrative reports are made up to record 'strictly municipal infringements'. Reports of 'mixed infringements' are still sent to the public prosecution agency. This procedure means there is no role for a municipal sanctioning officer. Devroe (2012: 434) interprets this as stemming from a strong belief in Liège in restorative policing, with a marked preference for warning rather than sanctions. This means that the MAS Act is hardly used as a repressive instrument in Liège. Strikingly, mediation as an element of the MAS procedure is rarely applied here. The general preference in Liège is for the traditional strategies of the police and the criminal justice agencies.

Evere (Brussels Capital Region)[43]

In the Brussels Capital Region, as in Wallonia, there are not many municipal governments that deploy community guard-recorders. One exception is the municipality of Evere (37,000 inhabitants[44]). This medium-sized municipality has twelve community guards, five of whom also have formal power as a recorder. One of the main reasons why the municipal authorities introduced community guard-recorders was that in their view the police were insufficiently involved in the policing of nuisance, disorder and petty crime, issues that worried many citizens. The municipal community guard-recorders fill the gap left by the police. The local government in Evere also assumes that the presence of community guards and community guard-recorders will reduce citizens' feelings of insecurity.

---

43 This section is mainly based on the interview with respondent 4 Belgium.

44 Website of the municipality of Evere: http://www.evere.be/index.php/nl/startpagina/voorstelling, retrieved 10 December 2012.

The community guards and community guard-recorders spend most of their time patrolling the streets. Work in their office to complete their paperwork takes only two or three hours a week. The guards wear the legally prescribed purple uniform. The work of community guards is mainly prevention-oriented. Guards with recording powers are supposed to use both preventive and repressive strategies. Prevention is mainly achieved through a visible presence near schools, both mornings and afternoons. The guards make sure everything runs smoothly, help children to cross the street and try to manage the traffic flows of parents picking up their children. At such moments the community guards will normally not make reports. However, at other times they are expected to be more repressive.

Their repressive activities focus on illegal dumping of garbage and other petty forms of environmental pollution, among other things. The municipality of Evere pays a great deal of attention to maintaining its image as a green residential area, where it is pleasant to live. Administrative fines for unacceptable behaviour such as illegal dumping are seen as having a strong symbolic function. On the one hand they should send the message that the municipal community wants to keep Evere a pleasant, green place to live. On the other hand, MAS fines should symbolize that local authorities care seriously about their citizen's worries.

Most of the MAS reports made out by community guard-recorders are accepted by the municipal sanctioning officer. Usually a proposal is made for mediation first (for example, community service). In case of repeat offenders or 'shocking incidents', mediation is abandoned and an administrative fine is levied.

For the past few years the numbers of MAS reports and sanctions have been rising in Evere. There were approximately 2,200 notifications in 2012.[45] Most reports in Evere are drawn up by the police.

The police and the community guard-recorders in Evere may cooperate in special campaigns (for instance, focusing on the prevention of car theft or illegal dumping). In such cases there may be joint briefings and joint patrols. Mainly for financial reasons the community guards and community guard-recorders in Evere do not normally have a direct line of communication with the police (radio or red button). In risky situations their calls to the police will be handled with high priority, in which case the police should arrive on the spot within a few minutes.

5.4 Private security officers in public space

In 2010 there were 15,411 licensed private security officers in Belgium (CoESS, 2011: 15). Private security in Belgium plays only a very limited role in the public space.[46] There is a general reservation with regard to private security. There is an

45 Estimated on the basis of data provided by the municipality of Evere.

46 Devroe (2012: 321); interviews with respondents 2 and 4 Belgium.

overwhelming consensus that surveillance and enforcement tasks in the public space should only be performed by state institutions. This is certainly also the predominant view concerning the use of coercion, which is seen as the uncontested monopoly of the state.[47] Given this consensus, a public debate about the use of private security in public space has never emerged (Devroe, 2012: 324-325). On the other hand, private security companies are certainly eager to take over the tasks of community guards, with and without formal powers.[48]
The limited role of private security in public space can be illustrated by the following example. One of the interviewees told us about some examples of private security in public space in Belgium. He mentioned as a significant example the city of Mechelen, where private security officers were contracted by owners of pubs and discotheques for surveillance tasks in the (public) entertainment area of Mechelen. Such patrols would be partly funded by the municipal government. It turned out that such a regulation does indeed exist in Mechelen. However, it was only used once, about five years ago, shortly after its introduction. Since that time it has become a 'paper reality', as a representative of the city of Mechelen described it to us.

Tasks, powers and requirements

In Belgium private security officers are only permitted to conduct surveillance tasks on public roads if they are guarding goods and persons (Devroe, 2012: 321-324).[49] Private security officers may also work on public transport and in access control (Cools & Verbeiren, 2008).
Private security guards working in the public space have no more powers than any other citizen. They have the power to hold a person who is caught in a criminal act, while awaiting the police. Any citizen in Belgium is authorized to take such action. Under certain conditions private security officers are permitted to do body searches in locations that are accessible to the general public. This is only permitted for security reasons, not to check for drugs.[50]
The Belgian Act on the Regulation of Private Security (1990)[51] introduced certain requirements for private security: all private security companies must have a licence, which is granted by the Minister of the Interior. Private security officers must also meet a number of requirements: they must be at least eighteen years

47 Interview with respondent 2 Belgium.
48 Interviews with respondents 1 and 3 Belgium.
49 'Memorie van Toelichting bij het wetsontwerp tot wijziging van de wet van 10 april en bij het wetsontwerp tot invoering van een artikel 117bis in de wet van 10 april 1990 op de bewakingsondernemingen en private bewakingsdiensten'. *Parl. St. Kamer*, 2002-2003, nr. 2328/1 en 2329/1, p. 5-6.
50 Interview with respondent 1 Belgium.
51 'Wet van 10 april 1990 tot regeling van de private en bijzondere veiligheid'. In: *Belgisch Staatsblad*, 29 May 1990.

old, resident of a Member State of the EU, without a criminal record, have a certain level of education and training, and they must not have been employed by the police during the previous five years. Moreover, the law states that private security officers should have *'respect for the fundamental rights of fellow citizens, have integrity, resilience regarding aggressive behaviour and self control, and no suspicious relations with a criminal environment'*.[52]
In Belgium private security officers have to take at least 132 hours of lessons. The training includes theoretical and practical elements. The topics covered include formal rules, rights and duties of private security agents, social skills and the ability to cope with stress and aggression. The training must be followed at a recognized institution.[53] Supervision of private security officers is the responsibility of the Ministry of the Interior. Important standards for the regulation of private security are the protection of privacy and fundamental citizens' rights.[54]

Equipment and uniforms

In Belgium private security guards may (in some cases 'should') wear uniforms in public and semipublic spaces. This uniform must not resemble the police uniform and must display an established insignia. Private security guards must carry an identification card while on duty.[55]
The Belgian Act on the Regulation of Private Security (1990) does not stipulate rules for the equipment of private security guards in the public space. Private security guards working on public transport are permitted to carry handcuffs. Handcuffs might only be used in cases of absolute urgency and only if no less intrusive methods are available. (Cools and Verbeiren, 2008: 9).

5.5 Relations with the police

Formally, the community guards, with or without a recording power, have to cooperate with the local police. Their relationship with the police must be based upon *'complementarity of tasks and an effective exchange of updated information'*. Because there has to be a clear distinction between the tasks of community guards and community guard-recorders and those of other security professionals, the community guards and community guard-recorders must be employed by a

52 Article 2, 6, 7 of the Act on the Regulation of Private Security (1990).

53 The Royal Decree 'K.B. van 18 juli 2008 tot wijziging van het Koninklijk Besluit, etc. van 21 december 2006.' In: *Het Belgisch Staatsblad*, 3 March 2008.

54 Ministry of the Interior: www.ibz.be/download/2011/jaarverslag-ibz-2011-web.pdf, retrieved 27 November 2012.

55 Article 8 of the Act Act on the Regulation of Private Security (1990) and the Circular 'Ministerieel besluit tot bepaling van het model van de werkkledij en het embleem van bewakingsagenten'. In: *Het Belgisch Staatsblad*, 8 June 2007.

municipal Service of Community Guards. The police are not permitted to supervise municipal guards. The authority and management of these guards, as well as the control and coordination of their tasks, is the sole responsibility of the municipal government.

Local authorities are also responsible for ensuring that the community guards and community guard-recorders perform their work in accordance with the law and formal regulations. Members of the police and officials appointed by the King are entitled to check whether community guards comply with formal standards, such as visibly wearing their identity card, showing respect for citizens, and not abusing their powers.[56]

Co-participation of police and community guards and community guard-recorders is permitted in the case of specific actions. However, mixed patrols where duties of the police and those of the community guards might be confused, are formally avoided. The cooperation between the municipal Service of Community Guards and the zonal police is laid down in a written agreement, which should also include the kind of information that can be exchanged.[57]

In practice the relations between the police and the municipal community guards are more wide-ranging and contradictory than these formal regulations may suggest. For instance, in Liège the police are very dominant, whereas in Antwerp the municipal administration is the central actor. Other municipalities have found a kind of middle course. In some cases a more integrated multi-agency approach exists; in other cases municipalities and police continue to operate in separate worlds, each with its own responsibilities.

5.6 Protection of citizens

The protection of citizens' rights with regard to Municipal Administrative Sanctions is regulated in both the MAS Act and the Ministerial Circular PREV 32 (2010). When the municipal sanctioning officer pronounces his sanction, he must also let the offender know that he/she has the right to defend him-/herself within a period of fifteen days. If an administrative fine higher than € 62.50 is imposed, the offender has the right to request a personal defence of his case. He has the right to be assisted or represented by a legal advisor and to examine relevant evidence. If the offender is under the age of eighteen, the president of the Bar Association must be informed, so that the offender may be assisted by coun-

56 Article 7 and 17 of the Community Guards Act (2007) and the Circular 'Ministeriële omzendbrief PREV 32' (2010).

57 'Ministeriële omzendbrief PREV 32' (2010). Also Articles 6 §3 and 15 of the Community Guards Act (2007).

sel.[58] In addition, citizens can initiate proceedings before the Council of State. In practice this rarely happens because of the burdens of this procedure on the offender.[59]

The Belgian Act for the Regulation of Private Security (1990) gives individual citizens the right to complain about the actions of private security guards. No individual citizen should be guarded without explicit permission.[60] In all cases it must be clearly stated that private security companies are working in a given area. This is indicated by a kind of traffic sign that announces the presence of private security officers.

As far as we could trace, the formal complaints procedures mentioned in this section are rarely used in practice. This applies both to the procedures concerning public guards and private security officers.[61] The only exception may be the right to mount a personal defence against a decision to issue a municipal administrative sanction.[62]

5.7 Debate

Plural policing is a matter of public debate in Belgium, with several issues dominating over the past few years. Some of these are briefly discussed below.

Private security officers in the public space

Over the past few years there has been a strong consensus in Belgium that private security should not take on any public tasks. The private security industry would be happy to engage in activities that hitherto have been done by municipal community guards, with and without recording powers. The private sector claims that it is well equipped to do this work, often more economically and efficiently. To counter fears that the private sector might undermine important public values, representatives of the sector claim that the governance and accountability of private security companies are much stricter than the regulation and control of public community guards.

The Belgian debate about private security officers in the public space is highly ideological in tone. Proponents and opponents are mostly divided along political lines. Generally speaking, the Social Democrats want to keep the public role of

58 Article 119bis of the New Municipal Act; and the Circular 'Ministeriële omzendbrief PREV32 (2010).

59 Interview with respondent 1 Belgium.

60 Article 8, §5 of the Act for the Regulation of Private Security (1990).

61 Interview with respondent 1 Belgium.

62 Interview with respondents 5 and 6 Belgium.

private security as limited as possible, whereas the Liberals do not appear to have many objections to expansion.[63]

There is a debate on two levels in Belgium about private security in the public space. First, in some cities and municipalities it is an issue that reappears on the agenda from time to time. However, it is also an issue that demands policy attention at the federal level. At both levels it seems that this debate deals not only with more ideological views on the role of the state or the relation between public and private sectors; it is also a debate that concerns economy, the need for austerity and potential cuts in public spending. At the same time it concerns the core tasks of the police, especially at the local level. What are seen as the proper local tasks of the police? And if the police are not able or willing to perform these tasks, will municipal authorities do them on their own? Do they use municipal community guards or do they contract private security officers, with the promise that the latter are more flexible and cheaper?[64]

Although this debate may be ongoing, the consensus in Belgium still seems pretty clear: private security should not have an important task in the public space. It looks as if this will not change in the near future.

Separation of powers[65]

For the past few years the procedures under the MAS Act have attracted a lot of criticism, whether from the academic world (Cops, Put and Pleysier, 2012), the judiciary,[66] or the Belgian League of Human Rights.[67] The main criticism is that there is one municipal officer (the community guard-recorder) who produces the administrative report, whereas another officer of the same municipal administration (the sanctioning officer) decides on the imposition of the administrative sanction. That means the municipal administration acts both as the recorder of the infringement, and as legislator, prosecutor, victim, decision maker and beneficiary (as the recipient of the fines). This is viewed as conflicting with the principle of the separation of powers. Some critics claim that the consequences of this failing separation of powers can already be seen: some local authorities frequently use the MAS Act for political reasons, for example against political demonstra-

63 Interviews with respondents 1 and 3 Belgium.

64 Interview with respondents 1 and 3 Belgium.

65 Interviews with respondents 1, 2 and 3 Belgium.

66 For an example: www.nieuwsblad.be/article/detail.aspx?articleid=FL3QJJVS, retrieved 5 December 2012.

67 The League has an action called: "GAS? No thanks!"; www.mensenrechten.be/index.php/site/nieuwsberichten/gas_icoon. www.mensenrechten.be/index.php/site/pagina/wie_zijn_we, retrieved 6 December 2012.

tions or the illegal fly-posting of posters with messages that are not complimentary to the local authorities.[68]
Another related question is whether local authorities should play any role as a sanctioning body. Some critics argue that sanctioning powers with regard to minors should lie only with the juvenile court. In the view of some local authorities, because the criminal justice agencies do not pay enough attention to petty juvenile cases, there seems to be some sort of impunity. As a result, local authorities feel compelled to take on a role for which they are not fit (sometimes even against their own views and preferences). These local authorities would be happy to give back this responsibility to juvenile criminal justice agencies (juvenile courts, child protection, etc.), but are afraid that this will not happen in the near future.[69]

Prevention or repression

After almost fifteen years there is still a debate in Belgium about the question whether the MAS Act and its implementation are preventive or repressive.[70]
One of the issues under discussion is whether it is possible to let one officer (the municipal community guard-recorder) engage in both prevention and repression. In this debate there is a clear difference between predominant views in Wallonia as opposed to Flanders. Whereas in Flanders the role of a community guard-recorder is more or less accepted, in Wallonia there is still a debate about the question whether a community guard who is involved in pronouncing sanctions is still able to do the preventive work adequately. In Wallonia there are fears that citizens will not understand this combination.[71]
In its '*MAS? No thanks!*' campaign the Belgian League of Human Rights argues that the MAS-Act disturbed the balance between prevention and repression and that there is too much emphasis on sanctions. This is not only a debate of principles, but also a question of the degree to which the assumption underlying the MAS system is correct, which is that the repressive nature of administrative sanctions will promote effectiveness (Cops, Put & Pleysier, 2012).

Lower age limit[72]

The age limit for persons who may be given a MAS sanction was recently lowered from sixteen to fourteen years. This measure gave rise to a lot of debate.

68 See for examples: www.dewereldmorgen.be/artikels/2012/03/08/gas-boetes-financieel-gewin-en-politieke-repressie, www.dewereldmorgen.be/foto/2012/03/12/occupy-antwerpen-en-de-gemeentelijke-asociale-straffen, both retrieved 5 December 2012.
69 Interview with respondent 2 Belgium.
70 Interview with respondent 4 Belgium. Also: www.urbansecurity.be/?/lang=nl, retrieved 12 December 2012.
71 Interview with respondent 4 Belgium.
72 Interviews with respondents 1, 2, 3 and 4 Belgium.

Both academics and representatives of the Flemish children's rights commission criticized the measure fiercely,[73] their main argument being that punishment is not appropriate for young people, and that the age limit should be raised. However, proponents of the lower age limit argue that there is a growing category of young offenders who are involved in serious forms of delinquent behaviour. For that reason it is viewed as necessary that even young persons should be treated as responsible for their own behaviour. Antwerp in particular produced strong advocates for a lower age limit. Their argument is that the main function of administrative sanctions is not so much to punish young people. Rather the MAS sanction can be used as a threat that should work as an incentive for young people to accept mediation or follow a course or receive social work assistance.

5.8 Conclusion

Belgium too has its plural policing. Since the 1990s, different forms of non-police policing officers have become visible on Belgian streets. This development was fuelled by four factors. First, many citizens were dissatisfied with the poor management of social disorder and petty crime. Second, partly because of the rise of the far-right nationalist political party Vlaams Blok, social-democratic local governments felt under pressure to demonstrate their decisiveness in the management of social disorder and petty crime, issues that prove to be important for the feelings of security of many citizens. Third, additional job creation programmes as an element of the Belgian security and prevention contracts paved the way for new jobs for guards, wardens and surveillance workers in the public space. Fourth, because the police and the public prosecution agency neglected the management of social disorder and petty crime, the MAS Act was introduced to allow municipal governments to tackle these problems themselves. Since 2007 – when community guards with recording powers were introduced – this system can be used more effectively. Nevertheless, there are striking differences in the implementation of the MAS Act and the use of these municipal enforcement officers, especially between Flanders and Wallonia/Brussels. The latter region has almost no community guard-recorders, whereas in Flanders they have acquired a generally accepted, quite strong position. Different views on the proper role of the state and especially of the police are relevant here, as are divergent notions about the importance of a local, integrated security policy. Finally, in Belgium private security guards play almost no role in surveillance and enforcement in the public space.

73 Children's Rights Commission: www.kinderrechtencommissariaat.be, retrieved 6 December 2012.

6 Canada – Ontario

Canada is a federal state with ten provinces and three territories. Each province exercises its own legislative authority in a constitutional framework. The provinces are led by a premier who heads a government; this provincial government is controlled by legislature. The provinces have jurisdiction over many matters, including the police. Canada (population 34 million) is a typical immigration country. The number of visible minorities has gradually increased, especially in the large cities and metropolises, where these groups constitute about half the population.

In 2010, the country counted about 70,000 police officers and 27,000 civilian staff (Statistics Canada, 2010). It is estimated that there are currently 140,000 registered private security guards.[1]

This chapter concentrates on the province of Ontario. In 2010 the province counted more than 26,000 police officers (civilian personnel not included) (Statistics Canada, 2010). In 2010 in Toronto – by far the largest city of Ontario (and Canada) – 5,800 police officers were employed, in addition to about 2,000 civilian staff members (TPS Planning for the Future, 2011: 195).

In Canada, the private security industry is larger than the public police at a ratio of about 2:1 (Law Commission, 2006: 25). The number of licensees, including in-house security personnel, declined drastically after the introduction of a licence requirement for private security personnel in 2009. In 2010 over 50,000 private security guards were registered in Ontario. In 2009 there were just over 66,000, although it should be noted that between 2006 and 2009 the number of private security guards had grown very quickly, even doubling (TPS Planning for the Future, 2011: 238).

The private security industry offers many services that are often related to enforcement and crime control: surveillance on foot, by bicycle or car, as well as undercover surveillance and gathering gang-related information. In addition, many corporations in Canadian cities hire security guards to enforce minor

1 www.securitydirectornews.com/public-sector/canada-expands-citizen%E2%80%99s-arrest-powers-private-security-personnel, retrieved 27 November 2012.

norms, such as nuisance by the homeless, loitering youths, and graffiti. Private security companies thus also carry out enforcement tasks in privately owned public space, where they have relatively far-reaching powers as private citizens and agents of the property owners. This chapter takes a closer look at the security company Intelligarde International, which promotes itself explicitly as 'The law enforcement company'. Rigakos (2002) speaks in this context of a 'new parapolice', but the term parasoldiers also seems applicable here. At the same time many (quasi-) public surveillance organizations are active. These include the Corps of Commissionaires, a non-profit organization that employs former members of the armed forces. In Toronto and other cities, in the context of paid duty policing, regular police officers are also hired to patrol on behalf of private parties and social organizations, such as sports clubs and special events. In this way the public police also operate in the security market.

Finally, Canada has other government-related occupations that take on surveillance in the public space, including special constables and by-law enforcement officers. Sometimes these people are also called parapolice officers. This chapter pays no attention to other enforcement groups, such as wildlife officers, park wardens and conservation officers. These groups enforce a wide range of provincial laws related to nature and the environment, traffic and alcohol.

The Canadian context of security and enforcement in the public space is complex, with many different professional groups involved. As stated, this chapter is limited to Ontario, but occasionally, for clarification, some findings related to other Canadian provinces or cities are presented. This chapter then deals with: the police system (6.2), the parapolice (special constables and by-law officers) (6.3), paid duty policing (6.4), private security guards employed within the public space and the regulation of this profession (6.5), the activities of the company Intelligarde International (6.6), the relationship with the public police (6.7), the protection of citizens against abuse of powers (6.8), and finally some relevant debates (6.9).

6.1 Police system

The Royal Canadian Mounted Police (RCMP), also known as 'Mounties' (in French: Gendarmerie Royale du Canada) is the federal police force of Canada. Mounties, when in ceremonial uniform, are noticeable for their Strathcona boots and wide-brimmed hats. The RCMP also undertakes (inter-)national police tasks such as cooperation with Interpol.

Under contract, the RCMP provides police tasks for some municipalities, regions and provinces other than in Ontario and Quebec. More than half the staff is employed on a contract basis. The RCMP provides its services, for example, in the large western province of British Columbia. Most Canadian provinces are legally required to provide police services, but they do not have to undertake

implementation themselves. Only Ontario, Quebec and Newfoundland & Labrador have their own provincial police, the Ontario Provincial Police (OPP), Sûreté du Québec, and the Royal Newfoundland Constabulary. The services of these forces are hired by (mainly sparsely populated) municipalities and regions. The large and medium municipalities all have their own police force. In addition, there is the so-called First Nations Policing, consisting of police agreements with aboriginal communities, which also have the option of establishing their own police services.
Canada has about 350 providers of police forces, including the RCMP, the OPP, and a large number of regional and municipal forces. The RCMP is the largest police force (in 2005 the service had approximately 22,500 police officers).[2]
The police system in Canada is described as decentralized, but police officers at the local level may belong to a provincial or national police force. After expiry of a contract a municipality may hire members of another police force. A municipality can even legally contract several police forces within its territory (not usually done). In this way a mosaic of police forces has arisen at the municipal level in Canada. These forces vary greatly in terms of size and operational expenses. One of the results of these developments is that the classical formula of 'single jurisdiction – single police service' has little significance any more (Rigakos and Leung, 2006).

Until the 1960s, the federal government paid most of the local and provincial police budgets in those communities where the RCMP provided local policing services, but step by step the municipalities had to pay much more. Nowadays the RCMP's target is 100% cost recovery: the contractors pay all costs themselves (Rigakos, 2002: 47). While the cost of the public police has continued to grow in recent decades, the number of uniformed public police officers per 100,000 population has declined since the 1990s. According to Rigakos and Leung (2006), the increasing costs of public police could be the reason for the rise of the private sector. The contract-based police arrangements between cities and provinces and the RCMP have led to the formation of regional units. This process of scaling up also occurred in Ontario (Lithopoulos & Rigakos, 2005). Whether this increase in scale actually leads to a more effective and efficient policy (as is claimed) is questionable: in terms of numbers of cases cleared and costs per officer, regional units do no better than smaller police forces (Lithopoulos & Rigakos, 2005).

The Police Services Act (PSA) of Ontario (1990) requires municipalities themselves to provide the police function. Every municipality is expected to pay for police forces itself and is obliged to weigh the pros and cons of having its own police or hiring police. There were considered to be two principal advantages to

2 The second largest force is the Toronto Police Service, followed by the OPP, the Sûreté du Québec and the Montreal Urban Community Police (Law Commission 2006; Rigakos & Leung, 2006).

this system: municipalities would accurately determine what specific kinds of services they need, and they would have the option to terminate services in case of poor quality (Law Commission, 2006: 51).
The OPP is involved in more than 300 contracts in which they provide police services to municipalities (ibid.). According to the Law Commission this contract business has led to a police market within the government sphere, whereby the police see themselves as suppliers of products; they have adopted a commercial language and management style (for example through the establishment of an annual business plan). Along with the rise of this business model within the police services there is a trend towards civilianization: civilian personnel carry out a progressively higher proportion of functions. This is a trend that has been ongoing for over thirty years.

The PSA indicates that police officers have a duty to maintain peace and to prevent crime (Section 42). Police officers are primarily peace officers. Furthermore, the Act provides that every municipal police force in Ontario must have a Police Services Board. In small municipalities the board comprises three people, including the mayor, an independent citizen and a person appointed by the province. In medium and large municipalities the number of members rises to five and seven, respectively. These boards develop police policies, set priorities, appoint staff, hire the police chief (and the deputy chiefs), and develop guidelines relating to public complaints. The operational management of the municipal police force is the responsibility of the service provider. Boards act as a buffer against politics, so that the political independence of the police can be better guaranteed (Law Commission, 2006: 85).[3]

The PSA of Ontario refers to the provision of police services. In consequence, there is no specific federal institution responsible for policing in general (Hermer et al., 2005: 32). Private providers of police services are regulated by legislation that refers to 'private security'. One of the implications of this system is that it is unclear where the responsibilities of the public police stop and where those of non-state police begin.

6.2 Parapolice

In Canada many uniformed enforcement officers perform tasks within the public space. Within the context of this study, the following parapolicing officers are important: the special constables and the by-law officers. In a sense, the Corps of

3 Respondent 1 points out that police services boards are less focused on the short term and keep political meddling at a distance.

Commissionaires can also be counted among these bodies, although the Commissionaires nowadays fall under private security legislation in each province.

Special constables

Special constables are often called 'parapolicing officers' (Carroll, 2004a; Rigakos & Leung, 2006).[4] They work, for example, on university campuses, in public transport, in government residential complexes, in airports, national and provincial parks and government buildings.

In Canada, in contrast to England & Wales, special constables are professional, sworn peace officers who are appointed by the local police services boards but employed by their own organizations. Their contract specifies the periods when they must operate, in which specific area, and the purpose of their activities. Mandate and powers are usually defined by agreement with the Board.[5]

Approximately 3,500 special constables are appointed in the province of Ontario. Most are employed by smaller municipalities (OACP, 2010).[6] The Police Services Act states that special constables within their territory may have full police powers, which means that as peace officers they can independently arrest and detain citizens, without involving the regular police, except for more serious offences. They have the authority to arrest persons on reasonable and probable grounds (under the Criminal Code) (Carroll, 2004a).

Special constables may also enforce provincial laws (such as liquor laws) and municipal by-laws. They often also undertake the task of crime fighting. They have no firearms, with the exception of the Niagara Parks Police (which consists entirely of special constables). The special constables are equipped with handcuffs, batons, sometimes pepper spray and they often wear body armour. Special constables receive a variety of training, depending on their contracts with the police. In Ontario, they are not subject to the public complaint system, nor the Special Investigations Unit (an independent body which oversees the police) (Carroll, 2004a).

4 Rigakos (2002) reserves the term 'new parapolice' for security officers who carry out public tasks, but are employed in the private security industry.

5 In Canada, the special constable does not refer to a police volunteer who in particular can be temporarily sworn-in in times of acute distress and can be added to the corps. Auxiliary constables operate in some cities: police volunteers who patrol in parks, for example. If they are accompanied by regular police officers they have the same police powers. Respondents who addressed this issue do not have the impression that policymakers have plans to expand this group (as is the case in England & Wales).

6 Numbers of special constables in Toronto: in 2010 74 special constables worked with the Toronto Transit Commission; Toronto Community Housing, which manages 60,000 housing units, employed 83 special constables (though provincial offences officers, parking enforcement officers and a Strategic Safety Team are also on the staff). 43 special constables were working at the University of Toronto in 2010. (Planning for the Future: 234 ff).

The Ontario Association of Chiefs of Police (OACP, 2010) has noted a lack of legislation on special constables and their tasks and responsibilities (lack of democratic oversight of the profession and lack of a public complaint system; lack of guidelines for uniforms and equipment; unclear rules on appointments, etc.). It is confusing that a special constable status can be granted powers similar to police and in some cases use the title 'police'. The respective responsibilities of those groups differ significantly from each other.

According to the OACP a dual police system has arisen in Ontario. As demand for police services has increased, with ever more swingeing cuts to the public police forces, boards are coming increasingly to rely on special constables (see also Law Commission, 2006).

Most respondents think the Ontario guidelines on special constables are not clear. Three of them point out that regulations in Alberta are better: minimum standards have been created for special constables including training, uniforms, and titles including prohibiting special constables from using the term 'police'. Alberta has established separate police ranks, together with corresponding activities.[7]

Special constables at universities

A university decides whether it wants a parapolice model or a private security one. Some universities (like the University of Toronto) adopted the first model many years ago, while other universities do not appreciate police-like security officers on the usually extensive campus areas. Depending on the policy of the university, the security staff consists of special constables or private security guards (in-house or contract security guards).

Canadian universities often have communities where many staff members, students and visitors stay for a long time. The University of Toronto (the largest in Canada, with 70,000 students) includes a large urban area with many streets, shopping centres, restaurants, bars, sports facilities and large parking lots.

Most universities define their security service as community-based and are thereby inspired by the principles of partnership, problem solving, ownership (responsibility for specific areas) and empowerment (informal leadership) (Carroll, 2004a).

The University of Toronto has a special constable model; personnel are explicitly presented as 'police'. The vehicles also bear the designation 'police'. The special constables are equipped with handcuffs and batons. Some special constables at other universities (and transit authorities) are also equipped with pepper spray. Requirements for training and equipment are stricter than for private security guards. Furthermore, private security guards can only make arrests as private

7 The Peace Officer Act was enacted in Alberta; Alberta peace officers do have limited police powers: level 1 peace officers have access to firearms; level 2 do not (see the Public Security Peace Officer Program, Government of Alberta).

citizens whereas special constables have the arrest authority of peace officers. The powers of special constables are also limited compared to those of the regular police.[8]

The University of Toronto campus employs 54 special constables. They are trained by a Campus Police Instructor. They are available 24/7 and patrol on foot, by bicycle or car. The Bicycle Unit comprises 20 employees. Besides the special constables, community safety workers are also appointed to carry out preventive work.[9]

By-law enforcement officers

By-law enforcement officers (in Ontario: municipal law enforcement officers) are authorized to enforce municipal laws relating to, for example, parking, noise nuisance, building codes, control of animals, and environmental protection. These officers enforce only certain types of infringement, falling under specific legislation. There were Animal Control Officers, Building Inspectors, etc. Initially, many municipal enforcement officers enjoyed barely any legal protection. Meter Maids imposed fines for unpaid parking. They were later renamed Parking Enforcement Officers.[10]

By-law enforcement officers are peace officers as defined in section 2 of the Criminal Code of Canada. The Police Services Act of Ontario states: *'Municipal law enforcement officers are peace officers for the purpose of enforcing municipal by-laws.'* Municipal law enforcement officers are sworn in as provincial offences officers, but not as special constables. The powers and equipment of by-law officers vary from municipality to municipality. They have the authority to issue summonses, to impose fines and collect data for the purpose of prosecution. They are not usually equipped with batons and pepper spray as they do have the authority to make arrests. The exact extent of their powers is unclear.

Private security personnel may be granted the status of provincial offences officer for specific and limited tasks. The peace officer status of security guards who are contracted by the municipality only applies to the enforcement of municipal or parking by-laws under the Provincial Offences Act.[11]

8 Respondent 6 says: *"We can only investigate and arrest and do other actions on our own territory. We are allowed to do full investigations on the lower level. We are not allowed to be engaged in serious crimes without backing up the police. We ensure the enforcement of theft under $ 5,000, but if it is more than that, the police should be called (...) We always inform the police if we take action within our mandate. But we arrest people, we examine them, we release people with a message when they have to appear in court, we impose fines. We cannot stop cars on the streets, that only the police can do."*

9 www.campuspolice.utoronto.ca/about-police.htm, retrieved 27 November 2012.

10 http://en.wikipedia.org/wiki/Bylaw_enforcement_officer, retrieved 27 November 2012.

11 Interview respondent 2. See also: http://en.wikipedia.org/wiki/Bylaw_enforcement_officer, retrieved 27 November 2012.

The Law Commission (2006) points out that by-law officers are cheaper than conventional public police (also Murphy and Clarke, 2005: 222). The officers can be used flexibly (but not 24/7 like the police) and deal with less serious matters. Little research has been done on by-law officers. Some respondents suggest that the public police would not be willing to enforce municipal regulations, partly because of budget cuts and the shift of the work to more serious matters.[12]

One of the respondents[13] points out that the City Administration of Hamilton (525,000 inhabitants) wants more by-law officers and special constables, to oversee relatively minor incidents. He is against this expansion for two reasons: first, their professional standards are too low and these two enforcement groups are not democratically accountable; secondly, both groups often act beyond their powers, as in Toronto where special constables also carry out investigative and undercover work. The respondent points out that the staff in many security companies are encouraged to follow a course for municipal law enforcement officers for parking enforcement purposes. Private security guards then obtain the power to impose parking fines, inter alia.

Corps of Commissionaires

According to Rigakos and Leung (2006) it is especially small municipalities that make use of members of the Corps of Commissionaires, who are authorized to enforce by-laws. The Corps is a not-for-profit organization consisting of persons who have previously been employed by the armed forces. In other words, they are not in the permanent employ of government institutions.

The Corps provides services to businesses, large organizations and the federal and provincial government. The biggest customer is the federal government. Legislation stipulates that departments have to consider the Corps' services first. This is known as the 'right of first refusal': contracts are first offered to the Corps. This right is reviewed by the Treasury Board every five years and may (possibly) be extended (Rigakos and Leung, 2006; see also Lippert and O'Connor, 2003).

This formula has provoked a great deal of criticism, especially from the security industry: it is said to lead to unfair competition because the Commissionaires are subsidized in the form of federal/military pensions. The benefit to the federal government is that costs can be kept low and use can be made of relatively well trained, certified personnel. Around 2000 about 11,000 Commissionaires were working in the security sector (Rigakos and Leung, 2006).

12 The exact number of by-law officers employed in municipalities within the province of Ontario is difficult to trace. The Municipal Law Enforcement Officers' Association of Ontario has more than 1,500 members. See www.mleoa.ca, retrieved 27 November 2012.

13 Interview respondent 3.

6.3 Paid duty policing

Another hybrid form of surveillance on the street is paid duty policing: sworn police officers providing services to private clients, such as policing at events and festivities. This is done in one of two ways: either by 'moonlighting' (also called secondary employment) whereby police officers work on behalf of private parties in their off-duty time. This is generally considered a dubious source of income and many forces do not permit it. The second form is paid duty work where the customer formally signs a contract with the force or the police union (although this also relates to off-duty hours). Thus stadiums such as Toronto's SkyDome can hire police officers on this basis. Citizens and private organizations can also hire police officers during events. Some local events fall under municipal by-laws whereby a permit is issued only on condition that paid duty personnel are hired. Although they are paid by private clients, municipalities remain responsible if officers act unlawfully (Law Commission, 2006: 52).

Paid duty officers can be hired for special events such as high school dances, Boxing Day retail sales, or major sporting events. Police officers may also be hired for a longer period, for example at airports. If the client wishes, police officers can be added to the security service of shopping malls (Carroll, 2004a).

According to one respondent, paid duty policing is big business. The personnel are relatively expensive and the annualized costs are at least 80,000 CAD, while security guards cost between 20,000 and 30,000 CAD. He points out that police officers do not accept all the work offered, for example they do not work as door staff or bouncers in nightlife areas. The security industry is against this system; they believe it is unfair competition.[14]

Paid duty policing in downtown Toronto

The Toronto Police Service works with a paid duty system whereby businesses, social organizations and citizens can hire off-duty officers. The work concentrates on traffic around road construction, building sites and festivities. Construction companies and public utilities are by far the largest clients. In 2009, approximately 3,700 police officers made use of this scheme. Together they generated over 24 million CAD in additional revenue. The Toronto Police Service received 3.5 million CAD in administrative payments (15% of revenues) and 1 million CAD in payments on rented equipment. A quarter of the demand comes from government-related organizations.[15] According to the Auditor General's report,

---

14 See www.cbc.ca/news/canada/montreal/story/2010/06/11/mtl-garda-montreal-police.html?ref=rss, retrieved 27 November 2012.

15 Auditor General, City of Toronto / Toronto Police Service, Police Paid Duty – Balancing Cost Effectiveness and Public Safety 2011. See www.toronto.ca/audit/2011/policeservice-mar23.pdf.

the management of the paid duty system is labour-intensive and expensive; the cost is approximately equal to the contributions collected.

Paid duty police officers work regularly in Business Improvement Areas (BIAs). One example is Downtown Yonge BIA (DYBIA) in the heart of Toronto, which includes about 1,400 companies (Rigakos and Leung, 2006). The DYBIA hired police officers for foot patrol services; the officers were required to report daily activities (shift reports), thereby providing a check on which companies and stores were faced with criminal incidents. Police officers also oversee shopping areas and report to private clients. In order to allow paid duty officers to exercise these enforcement functions, the Metropolitan Toronto Police demanded that the shop owners confirm in writing that the police officers act as representatives of the private owners. According to Rigakos and Leung (2006), this represents a revolutionary development in the history of the Canadian police.
A later report on DYBIA (Rigakos, 2011) makes it clear that the paid duty officers have been replaced by private security officers, paid by the City of Toronto. This radical policy change was the result of a bloody shootout between gangs on Yonge Street (resulting in the murder of the student Jane Creba) and a changed management vision of the TPS.

Paid duty policing in Montreal

Paid duty policing has not been thoroughly studied in Canada, but a recent investigation into the commercialization of security within the Montreal Police Service (MPS) has been published (Mulone, 2012). Since 1999 the force has had a department to sell services and products (business development section). The department is part of the strategic plan to accommodate financial cuts and to increase the capacity of the organization. The goal is not to make profit, but to regain more control over Montreal's own territory.
According to Mulone (2012) not all services are available in the MPS supermarket (such as investigation and tackling serious crime). There are four categories of product and/or service on offer: training, consultation, rental of police equipment, and (most lucrative) hiring agents to patrol, guard and escort. Any organization or citizen can hire police officers for a minimum of four hours. One can hire a foot patrol, as well as car patrols and even a dog squad. The contract is sent out after a brief investigation, in which the applicant's background is checked.
According to Mulone, the range of products and services provide relatively little benefit to the police force: in 2009 it amounted to 4.7 million CAD, less than 1 per cent of the total budget. Nevertheless, the trend towards commercialization continues, Mulone states. Many critics have questioned this development, including its impact on police work and on the equitable distribution of security work throughout the territory. The police have identified the potential drawbacks to

its image and have curtailed the paid duty system as follows. First, police officers may be removed from their tasks at any time to provide emergency aid. Secondly, only off-duty police officers can be deployed for commercial services; police officers can thus not be compelled to perform commercial tasks. And thirdly, it is preferred to deploy special employees, including cadets who have not finished their training.

The MPS has thus become a major player in the security market: it can react flexibly to market fluctuations (temporary deployment of services). The paid duty system would increase the competitive power of the police (Mulone, 2012).

6.4 Private security in public and semipublic space

The Canadian security industry has gained in strength in recent decades. The industry offers a wide range of services, from forensic investigation to bodyguard services and access control. On the one hand there is a growing contract sector, including security services, personal security, security transports, consultants, private investigators, and personnel who build and manage alarm systems. The government is a major client in that sector. In addition, the in-house security industry has also expanded.

Security guards can perform relative simple tasks such as guarding construction sites, but they can also be used for more complex tasks such as dealing with disturbances, drunks and mentally disturbed persons, traffic incidents, providing medical assistance, and responding to fire alarms. Security guards may be authorized to carry firearms under special circumstances (e.g. armoured car personnel). Security guards are mostly called security officers, although the name is legally not permitted in Ontario (Carroll, 2004b). Within the law, 'company security officers' should only act on the property of clients and not on the street. Nevertheless, many employees who work in the public space tend to take pride in the title 'security officer', disdaining the label 'guard'.[16]

Mass private property has grown rapidly in the major cities since the 1960s. Many people use these areas not only for shopping but also for entertainment and all kinds of (commercial) services. Typically, large malls are guarded by security guards, but as stated above, paid duty officers may also be appointed. Often there is also a police station on the location. It also happens that paid duty officers patrol together in a team with security guards in some malls. In the West Edmonton Mall in Alberta, the largest mall in Canada, the security service processes some 40,000 notifications a year. 50 security guards are employed there, who take on many tasks, including surveillance on foot, by bicycle or car, as

16 www.securitymagazine.com/articles/83657-security-officers-how-changing-titles-changes-perceptions and www.canadiansecuritymag.com/Guarding/Editorial/The-language-police-come-to-Alberta.html.

well as undercover surveillance to trace multiple offenders (Murphy & Clarke, 2005: 243).

Shopping malls typically use private security contracts. An important task of security guards is to remove youngsters. The way they are removed varies greatly. Sometimes it is after a verbal order, and sometimes by written notification for a certain period (Manzo, 2004).

The number of Business Improvement Areas (BIAs) has also increased in recent decades. In 2006 there were 230 in Ontario (Rigakos and Leung, 2006).[17] BIAs are typically created by the local government to improve businesses' prospects (often to prevent consumer flight to suburbs), including the refurbishment of streets and the construction of parking lots. Usually, BIA associations contract private security guards, especially to combat antisocial behaviour (Law Commission, 2006; Mopas, 2005).

In addition to security guards, there are also community service representatives and city ambassadors active within BIAs (but not in Ontario). Municipalities often hire these persons. Their role is that of caretakers and public information providers (Hermer et al., 2005). Ambassadors wear distinctive uniforms that embody a 'clean & safe' image and they are thus clearly visible. The tasks of ambassadors include hospitality and encouraging consumption, but they also have tasks that focus on keeping the environment clean, addressing beggars and homeless persons, and reporting incidents like theft and drunkenness to the police (Sleiman & Lippert, 2010; Lippert, 2012). Vancouver security guards may be deployed as ambassadors (Huey et al., 2005).

In (usually) affluent neighbourhoods residents regularly hire a private firm to provide security patrols. Because of poor service and the atomized nature of fleeting private auspices, neighbourhood-initiated private security programmes, are unlikely to proliferate in Canada (Brown & Lippert, 2007).

One of the respondents[18] indicates that the growth of mass private properties has had major consequences. A great demand arose for the enforcement of relatively minor offences, often in the broad 'middle ground' where night watchmen no longer suffice. The public police was reluctant, in his opinion, to do surveillance work in this domain, partly due to pressure from the unions. According to this respondent, you do not need a fully equipped police officer costing 120,000 CAD in this new field. The last thing the unions would allow is underpaid, poorly trained people.

The 'middle ground', in his words, is almost completely colonized by security companies. Another aspect is that many senior employees of the public police

17 According to respondent 5 BIA's are no longer growing strongly. Funds are insufficient, and a large group of shop owners do not see much in the recruitment of security guards (or they withdraw their payments).

18 Interview with respondent 5.

are switching to the private industry, often in the last decade of their career; they start working as a security manager, but they often do their work as a public officer with a lot of emphasis on law enforcement. In this respondent's opinion, it is not surprising that people are arrested daily in many major malls. This also has to do with the scale of the malls. As an example consider Eaton Mall in Toronto, which has over 30 million visitors a year. It employs 15,000 people; the mall is much larger than many municipalities.

According to this respondent,[19] the educational level of the security guards is poor. One of the problems is that there is no differentiation in law of private security guards. Every jurisdiction in Canada has only one licence category, namely that for security guards. This means that guards who perform enforcement tasks in the public space are in exactly the same licence category as those who guard industrial sites.

This respondent states that there is little agreement about the standards of training. Bringing together all the different industries in one category is impossible in his view. In addition, most companies do not want additional costs for training; they want the cheapest employees. Therefore, according to this respondent, there is great resistance to regulation in the private security industry.[20]

Regulation: new legislation

Nevertheless, many things have changed in recent decades. After the Patrick Shand scandal in 1999 (a suspected thief who died while he was held captive by a security guard and two employees of a large grocery store chain in a Toronto mall) there was a great deal of commotion about the lack of regulation (Rigakos & Leung, 2006: 135; Law Commission, 2006: 101). Since then many statements, reports and recommendations on regulation of the sector have been published, including an influential report by the Law Commission of Canada (2002). The political pressure on the industry has grown.

According to the Law Commission, self-regulation is poorly developed within the industry and it contributes little to increased responsibility (2006: 103). Civil law is regularly used in practice, but criminal prosecution is rare (ibid: 102).

The Private Security and Investigative Services Act (2005) has introduced several changes in Ontario. First, a consistent basic training is mandatory for all security personnel. Secondly, a licence is required for all personnel, including in-house personnel and the Corps of Commissionaires. Thirdly, stricter conditions are imposed on uniforms, vehicles and security personnel's equipment. The province has been empowered to revoke licences in cases of unlawful behaviour or violation of the conditions (Law Commission, 2006: 100). The new Act aims to increase public confidence in the industry.

19 Interview with respondent 5.

20 Interview with respondent 5.

The Act was passed between 2007 and 2010, involving the code of conduct, criminal records checks, equipment, use of animals, data collection, registration requirements, and licence terms. The mandatory licence was implemented in 2008, including requirements relating to insurance for contract companies, and the requirements for uniforms and vehicles followed in 2009. Any new licence holder must have completed a training course, consisting of a minimum of 40 hours (basic training). In cases of complaints, the province may impose fines or revoke the licence.

As mentioned, more than 55,000 licences were issued in 2010, which represents a 16% decrease compared to 2009, when 66,000 people licensed. This decrease is due to the training requirement and the test for new licence applicants, and a mandatory test for existing licence holders. In 2010 there were still 75% more licence holders than in 2001, however (TPS Planning for the Future, 2011).

The programme has led to little improvement so far. According to one respondent, in practice, only a poor education is required: a small multiple choice test which everyone can pass.*"Standards are a joke!"* In addition, the department tasked with enforcing the new legislation is *"hilariously understaffed"* with only five field inspectors employed by the province. Security companies, according to this respondent, are not afraid of this new legislation and its enforcement. They are, however, afraid of bad publicity caused by tort law and 'getting fitted up'. All in all, there are few incentives to uphold law-abiding behaviour.[21]

Another respondent points to a related problem: security firms can circumvent the required licence by saying they do not have security personnel, but that they have, for example, hospitality employees. The new legislation, according to this respondent, has probably eliminated the 'lower bad layer' of the security industry: companies at the lower end of the market where wages are low and many immigrants are employed.[22]

According to some respondents the new legislation has not materially changed the abuses surrounding the actions of security guards in the public space. One respondent[23] points out that wrongful arrests, excessive force, removing homeless and illegal body search is still common. Another problem has to do with the fact that the police do not always take over arrested persons, because they have little time. As a result, many citizen's arrests are handled by telephone.

Citizen's arrest and private security

According to the Law Commission (2006), private and public officials are increasingly carrying out similar tasks and thereby frequently working together. Many

21 Interview with respondent 5.
22 Interview with respondent 3.
23 Interview with respondent 5.

security guards undertake public surveillance, communicate with citizens and are involved in arrests and body searches.
Many problems occur during these activities. Sometimes security guards who perform these public functions have only a minimum educational qualification, have had little training and have difficulty communicating in the English or French language (as the case may be) (Carroll, 2004b). Security guards also can perform and arrest relatively easily, because less evidence is required (Hermer et al., 2005: 48).
Private security guards have the same powers as ordinary citizens and the owners or operators for whom they work (Law Commission, 2006: 66). The power of citizens to arrest other citizens comes from the common law, but is today vested in Section 494 of the Criminal Code.[24] Everyone is entitled to arrest a person who has committed a prosecutable offence, or any criminal offence on or in relation to his or her property. The suspect must be immediately handed over to a peace officer (Law Commission, 2006: 67). The Criminal Code also indicates that the removal of a suspicious person at the insistence of the owner or his representative is allowed.
The provincial Trespass to Property Act also allows the arrest of suspects and their removal from the private domain. The owner or his representative is obliged to hand over the arrested person to the police. Although the provincial laws do not authorize the use of force in a citizen's arrest, the courts have determined that using necessary force is an implicit part of making an arrest (Law Commission, 2006: 68).
This Act gives security guards powerful tools to stop, question, remove or secure persons who exhibit problematic behaviour and commit offences on private property. Security guards thus have great discretionary leeway, which often conflicts with the freedoms and rights of citizens.

The traditional allocation of rights to private owners has major consequences for policing (Hermer et al., 2005). First, police officers have limited authority to enter private domains without the consent of the owner, property manager or a court order. On the other hand, the owner has the right, in person or through a representative (i.e. the appointed security guard), to check the behaviour of visitors on their own territory and to protect the area against unauthorized entry and, if

24 Title 494 reads as follows: *'Arrest without warrant by any person. (1) Any one may arrest without warrant: (a) a person whom he finds committing an indictable offence; or (b) a person who, on reasonable grounds, he believes (i) has committed a criminal offence, and (ii) is escaping from and freshly pursued by persons who have lawful authority to arrest that person.*
Arrest by owner, etc., of property (2) Anyone who is (a) the owner or a person in lawful possession of property, or (b) a person authorized by the owner or by a person in lawful possession of property, may arrest without warrant a person whom he finds committing a criminal offence on or in relation to that property.
Delivery to peace officer (3) Anyone other than a peace officer who arrests a person without warrant shall forthwith deliver the person to a peace officer.'

necessary, take coercive action against unauthorized persons. Unlike the actions of police officers (Charter of Rights and Freedoms: requirement for an 'articulable cause') the actions of private security guards are relatively little restricted by law. There are decisions of courts in which the homeowner, within the context of trespass law, is entitled to apply a reasonable degree of force during an arrest.[25]

In short, when it comes to freedoms and rights of citizens in the public domain, the court is usually strict: the Charter of Rights and Freedoms allocates less scope for intervention to the police. However, when it comes to private and quasi-public domains, judges are reluctant to protect civilians (Hermer et al., 2005: 36). In practice, this often means that security guards can remove citizens from the terrain in which they do surveillance work, and they do not have to give any reasons for doing so. If they had removed persons on grounds of discrimination, it would be difficult to prove. Matters are different for police officers and special constables: they must explain why, and they have to read the suspects their rights. There must be suspicion first, before an arrest.[26]

Bill C-26

Recently, the government passed a new Act, The Citizen's Arrest and Self-Defence Act, the aim of which is to better protect citizens when they proceed to arrest a person on their own domain. The citizen's arrest is extended and should now take place 'within a reasonable time after the offence is committed and they believe on reasonable grounds that it is not feasible in the circumstances for a peace officer to make the arrest'.[27]

The incentive for this new act was the Chen case: a shopkeeper in Toronto was charged with assault because he had overpowered and tied a thief up after he had stolen plants from the Lucky Moose Food Mart in May 2009. His 'mistake' was that he had acted a few hours after the incident. Under the old legislation, an arrest would only be possible if it followed immediately after the act had occurred. The new legislation, however, allows a suspect to be arrested 'within a reasonable time'.

The new Act is controversial and many fear that people may take the law into their own hands. It is theoretically possible that a security guard who witnesses a robbery by a group of men and who has no sufficient backup at that time, will look for the suspects with colleagues a few hours later in order to arrest them. Another possibility is that security guards will proceed to arrest a few days later, on the basis of CCTV images. It is unclear how the phrase 'within a reason-

25 RSO 1980 c511: *'a person authorized by the occupier (of a premise) may arrest without warrant any person he believes on reasonable and probable grounds to be on the premises....'*

26 Interviews with respondents 1, 3 and 4 Canada – Ontario.

27 Section 3 (1) of the 'Citizen's Arrest and Self-defense Act', replacing subsection 494(2) of the Criminal Code.

able time' can be explained and how much latitude judges will afford security guards. One of the possible risks is that people who have nothing to do with the (alleged) offence will be arrested.[28]

6.5 Intelligarde International

Many managers of housing complexes hire private security for surveillance, enforcement and crime fighting. Due to lack of manpower in the street, the public police cannot always provide such services, even in the most insecure areas. It is precisely in these neighbourhoods that use is often made of security companies.

Intelligarde International is a company that performs these surveillance and enforcement tasks. Ross McLeod, an eccentric sociologist and criminologist, also head of the Association of Private Security Agencies in Canada, founded the company in the early 1980s. When the company began, there were few arrests of suspects by security guards. In those early days many Intelligarde employees ended up in jail after arresting civilians. McLeod then managed to convince the police that his staff were entitled to use the citizen's arrest.[29] According to McLeod, policemen act as 'distant technocrats' who are unable to meet the needs of citizens. Against the background of dissatisfaction with the way the police worked in disadvantaged neighbourhoods, coupled with the political wind of zero tolerance, Intelligarde stepped into the enforcement field and presented itself explicitly as 'The Law Enforcement Company'. McLeod tries to convince local boards that they can outsource police work related to nuisance and petty crime (Tier II) to his company. At the same time, he emphasizes that his company contributes to community-based policing (Rigakos, 2002: 154).

Intelligarde employs about 700 people, not only in Toronto, but also in, for example, Hamilton and Ottawa. In Toronto the company has contracts with City Home Properties, a publicly funded housing association; the Metropolitan Toronto Housing Association; the Toronto Economic and Development Cooperation; Peel Living; and Toronto Parking Authority. In addition, the company does surveillance work within the port district and many commercial districts. A signifi-

28 www.securitydirectornews.com/public-sector/canada-expands-citizen%E2%80%99s-arrest-powers-private-security-personnel, retrieved 27 November 2012. See also: www.canadiansecuritymag.com/Risk-Management/Editorial/Why-the-citizen-s-arrest-policy-needs-to-be-revised.html.

29 www.securitydirectornews.com/public-sector/canada-expands-citizen%E2%80%99s-arrest-powers-private-security-personnel, retrieved 27 November 2012. McLeod is simultaneously a proponent of social work and community-based policing. In his view, enforcement and community development should ideally correlate. He opposes major international security companies with their ever-changing owners, which do not have 'institutional memory', or much knowledge of policing (see also McLeod & Saville 2012).

cant part of the Toronto downtown area (three square kilometres) is guarded by Intelligarde. More than 30,000 low-income tenants have to do with Intelligarde staff (Law Commission, 2006: 43). Intelligarde guards keep an eye on homeless people, drug users, prostitutes and gang-related activities. The company has its own database of persons with an area exclusion order.

Intelligarde has several units to meet a variety of needs[30]:
- *Uniformed*. This unit consists of high profile, proactive security guards. They control access to certain areas, maintain order, enforce laws, conduct safety checks and answer alarm notifications;
- *Mobile*. This team removes people from the street and inspects certain areas from plain (unbadged) cars; the team responds to alarm notifications;
- *Dog squad*. These teams are available in high-risk areas where employees often work alone, such as surveillance in parking areas;
- *Mounted*. These teams act during ceremonies and have other public functions.

According to the company, personnel receive training from experts, so they are able to acquire the same skills as public police officers. They also learn how to subdue and arrest an offender. Personnel wear bulletproof vests and special uniforms, very similar to the public police.[31] The employees are instructed to ask suspects three times to leave the area before proceeding to an arrest (Rigakos, 2002: 49). The suspect must then be surrendered to the police. Often the police release the suspects once again, which often leads to tensions with the security guards.
In the case of (alleged) nuisance, security guards often impose Notices Prohibiting Entry (NPEs) (shop / area exclusion orders) (Rigakos, 2002: 51). Intelligarde personnel impose thousands of NPEs per year, on the basis of which, according to Rigakos, it is easier to arrest suspects after a second or third incident. Intelligarde staff photograph each suspect and their data are stored in a database.
The staff are reluctant to engage in body search and seizure, due to formal problems if they do not have the suspect's consent. In practice, however, the uniform and appearance of authority are usually sufficient to obtain the suspects' consent. The staff are instructed to leave all items, except weapons, in the suspects' clothing. When the police arrive, they can alert them, for example, to drugs in a pocket.

Rigakos examined the extent to which the Intelligarde staff report incidents, receive complaints from citizens and become entangled in dangerous situations. Across the board, Intelligarde personnel score higher than police officers from the TPS. The higher level of reporting, according to Rigakos, can be explained by the fact that Intelligarde staff also act on minor offences, which police officers

30 www.intelligarde.org, retrieved 27 November 2012.
31 See 'A day in the life of an Intelligarde Officer', www.calgary-clic.ca/Resources/Documents/CSOs, retrieved 27 November 2012.

tend to ignore. Moreover, the Intelligarde guards – compared to police officers – have a three times greater chance of complaints being made against them. Rigakos points out that this has to do with the fact that the staff are also responsible for raids on drug houses, arresting drug users, and 'clearing' the street. In such cases they can be relatively quickly accused of racism or 'Gestapo tactics' (Rigakos, 2002: 59). Finally, Intelligarde employees are five times more likely to get involved in violence. Partly due to their lack of authority and status, security guards have many difficulties with non-cooperating suspects and angry bystanders. Backup in dangerous situations is thus central to the Intelligarde professional code. Rigakos in this context refers to a 'swarm or be swarmed professional ethos' (ibid: 60).[32]

The Intelligarde staff concentrate on noise nuisance, fights and violence, theft, and especially the removal of homeless people. The last is almost always accompanied by an arrest, but the police are called upon in only a quarter of all such cases. The police are most frequently called upon in cases of burglary, violence, theft, and drug related incidents (ibid: 61). Not surprisingly, Intelligarde has a bad reputation in the areas where the company operates. Citizen organizations have repeatedly launched a campaign against Intelligarde's 'attack on the poor' (ibid: 89).

According to Rigakos (2002), companies like Intelligarde arrest more people annually than many police forces in rural Ontario or in the suburbs. Companies such as Genesis in Vancouver also sell themselves as policing companies, with an aggressive reputation. City administrations accept this because they are cheaper.[33]

6.6 Relations with the police

In Toronto, cooperation between the police and private security is encouraged. The Toronto Association of Police and Private Security (TAPPS) is a public-private, not-for-profit partnership, with the aim of improving safety and quality of life in the city. TAPPS facilitates education, training, information, and the

32 Respondent 3 said about this during the interview: *"For example, they did the policing of Toronto Community Housing Corporation and scary things happened there. The public police will not enter that area unless they are in pairs. There they put down an unarmed private security officer to intervene in an incident. The guy only has a radio and maybe has handcuffs. It is therefore not surprising that there are risks."*

33 Respondent 6 in particular underlines that security officers are cheaper: *"The business improvement centre in the city here hired Intelligarde to patrol the streets (...) The added value is visibility, they behave as if they have powers, they call the police if you do bad things. That's basically it. They have done a good sales job."* According to respondent 1, many security officers are not 'intervention capable', although Intelligarde staff put a lot of work into training. Respondent 3 indicates that you can see a shift to more interventions and arrests when you look at the entire security industry in Canada.

exchange of data.[34] Within the partnerships, the importance of community policing is always endorsed, including areas such as large malls and the BIAs. The mall is perceived as a 'community', which is not surprising since numerous public institutions are usually housed there.[35]

The public police in many cases establish branch offices in large malls. This symbolizes that the public police and private security staff share responsibility for the same area. The informal exchange of information between both parties (including photos of suspects) is facilitated by the fact that many security companies are staffed by former police officers (Rigakos, 2002: 47).[36]

Security guards often work together with the police in 'sting operations', for example to combat theft in parking areas, and make official reports, for example in cases of theft and vandalism. In Vancouver loss prevention officers report to the Crown counsel with a request to proceed with prosecution, a task that was previously limited to peace officers (Huey, 2005: 162 ff). Many municipalities have strategic partnerships with private security companies. For example, security guards enforce municipal parking ordinances.

Some respondents observe that there are limits to the exchange of information on grounds of privacy legislation. The police do not always trust security guards. The police therefore exercise a degree of restraint.[37] One of the respondents has reservations about cooperation between police and other security personnel, even if they are by-law officers. Within each organization, he states, the organization's own interests and activities are given priority, while mutual understanding and common goals are needed for partnerships.[38]

6.7 Protection of citizen's rights

The public police can be held responsible in various ways. In Ontario, a Special Investigations Unit is responsible for supervising the police. In 2009 the Office of the Independent Police Review Director was added, which deals with complaints

34 According to respondent 1, cooperation is not encouraged in all police forces.

35 In a PowerPoint presentation of the Toronto Police Service as part of the Toronto Association of BIAs it is stated that: 'Helping to build safe communities is a sound business practice and can increase profit margins.' www.toronto-bia.com/resources/presentations/community_policing.ppt, retrieved 27 November 2012.

36 According to some respondents, the team approach in malls has its advantages. For example, the police are relieved when security companies provide information and carry out arrests (respondent 1). Security officers act as eyes and ears for the police; thanks to their camera systems much evidence goes to the police (respondent 2). Respondent 3 believes that the police see private security as a little brother who regularly needs help. Companies in turn are proud to be working with the police and frequently exchange information as they share broadcast frequencies.

37 Interviews with respondents 1 and 5.

38 Interview with respondent 2.

from citizens. Nevertheless, the Ombudsman of Ontario has questioned the current functioning of police supervision (Scott, 2012).

The protection of citizens against guards is still a hot issue in Canada. There is a vacuum in the regulation of surveillance work by security guards. This is troublesome because the performance of security guards increasingly involves enforcement work. As discussed above, provincial legislation on licences was recently significantly revised. Under the same legislation, citizens can now submit complaints about guards, but the provincial authorities cannot put a lot of work into dealing with these complaints, due to understaffing. There are few actual possibilities for the Ontario authorities to investigate the companies. One respondent indicated that the authorities have wide powers, like the ability to raid and seize the books, but this almost never happens.[39]
Citizens can still initiate a lawsuit in the case of abuse of powers or unlawful action by private security guards.

The Law Commission (2006: 74) concludes that the time has come for serious regulation of the performance of security guards, in both criminal and civil cases, especially in regard to arrest and detention. The problem is that security guards and citizens belong to the same legal category, regardless of the police work of the former group. Partly for this reason, judges continue to speak out against specific requirements for security guards. Apart from that, in Quebec security guards are expected to respect the Quebec Charter of Human Rights and Freedoms (ibid, 2006: 75).

6.8 Debate

The foregoing illustrates that functions of the police and security industry in Canada have increasingly spilled over and intermixed. In fact, in many respects security employees act as police officers in the public space and not as guardians. The security guards of Intelligarde carry out interrogation, arrests, and body searches. They are part of public crime control. Intelligarde security guards and public police officers come into contact with the public in the same ways. However, traditionally guards are not expected to deal with the public; they confine themselves to observing and reporting to their client.
Both public and private employees enforce rules and arrest citizens. Apart from the question whether security staff are always 'intervention capable', this raises many questions about democratic accountability. Burbidge (2005) puts that into focus in his study of the 'governance gap': it is unacceptable that the public police must answer to democratic bodies, while security officers perform the

39 Interview with respondent 3.

same work and are not subject to that constraint. One of the respondents says in this context that the biggest problem is that there is a rapidly growing middle group of security guards without any regulation. In his view, it is a failure that a second layer of public officials has not been introduced.[40]

Burbridge believes that Canada needs to work towards a model that includes both private and public police. Thus, there would be no space for a separate private policing governance structure. Many lawyers and criminologists endorse this idea (Cukier et al., 2003; Rigakos & Greener, 1999; Law Commission, 2006). The Charter of Rights and Freedoms offers protection only against government action. Generally, judges do not recognize the new situation of security guards performing police work; they adhere to a reduced level of constitutional protection against security guards.[41] The Canadian respondents also endorse the desirability of integrated legislation:

> 'I think we need one organizing body that regulates all types of police, public, private and hybrid. The plural approach is no problem for me, but as long as the parties are accountable to a Police Authority which has jurisdiction over them.'[42]

Another respondent points out:

> 'We must get rid of the mentality that private policing is a private matter. Security staff have to deal with many individuals and democratic supervision of this is in my opinion essential, as a first step. Arresting is a public matter, because you're doing it in the name of the state.'[43]

A related point is the commercialization of policing. The Law Commission (2006: 37) indicates that policing is becoming increasingly like an item of merchandise. According to Rigakos and Leung (2006), the interconvertibility of, for example, private security work and paid duty policing in public space creates an atmosphere of heightened competition and commercialization. This competition is also visible between public police forces when they try to gain contracts with municipalities, and between security companies and the public police. Local police service boards also have recourse to private security companies to perform additional police tasks, such as the enforcement of municipal by-laws (Rigakos & Leung, 2006: 136).

40 Interview with respondent 5.
41 For jurisprudence related to arrests of citizens by security guards, see Rigakos and Greener, 1999.
42 Interview with respondent 3.
43 Interview with respondent 4.

6.9 Conclusion

In the Canadian context, it is increasingly difficult to draw a dividing line between private and public responsibilities. It is not true that the private police simply fill the gap left behind by the public police. Neither can it be argued that private and public institutions are increasingly hostile to each other. In many cases there are overlapping, complementary activities (Law Commission, 2006). A large number of organizations and professional groups are responsible for surveillance work in the public space. Sometimes security guards are contracted by the public police, and private security guards sometimes handle complaints that were previously the exclusive domain of the public police. Sometimes companies hire public police officers to do surveillance in large shopping malls.

Police organizations can be placed on a continuum, with at one end public police forces controlled by democratic bodies, and at the other end security companies that guard private spaces such as shops and industrial sites. In between, many organizations operate, with an ambiguous status between public and private. For example, in the case of surveillance in BIAs, public interests and private interests are difficult to disentangle. For these reasons, it often seems odd to attribute separate forms of responsibility to private and public security workers.

If we look strictly at the 'middle ground' of enforcement (nuisance and minor offences), we can see that security companies have occupied most of that domain. The number of special constables and by-law officers carrying out surveillance work in this domain is probably quite small, although the number is increasing because they are cheaper than regular police officers.

7 Conclusion

The preceding chapters have analysed the rise, position and context of non-police providers of policing in five countries: the Netherlands, England & Wales, Austria, Belgium, and Canada (especially the province of Ontario). This study shows that, considered from an international comparative perspective, plural policing is a highly complex, disparate phenomenon. There are significant differences between these countries in their non-police providers of policing: these may be called wardens, city guards, patrollers, security officers, special investigative officers, surveillance officers and enforcement workers, or something different. It is not only the names given to these officers that differ, so do their tasks, formal powers, relations with the police, their legal basis, and the legal and social context within which they operate. Major differences may also be found between public and private providers and the authority under which they act, the circumstances that contributed to the introduction and rise of such wardens and enforcement officers, and in their governance. The countries also differ in the problems raised by the pluralization of policing and in the debate about such non-police policing officers in the public space. Plural policing also differs in respect of countless other, minor issues, such as their equipment, uniforms, and requirements for training and educational level, the organizational context in which the wardens and officers work, and the means of control and communication at their disposal.

The picture sketched here is very complex, not only because the differences between the countries are so significant; there are also marked differences within the countries between several types of wardens, guards and enforcement officers. There are often fundamental differences, even in one country, in their formal powers, social position, relations with the police and tasks undertaken. One of the factors contributing to this diversity and complexity is that the introduction, position and daily operations of these wardens, guards and enforcement officers is, to a significant degree, a local phenomenon. Even if there is regulation by the national government, nevertheless there are often important discrepancies between the policy and regulations at the national level, and their interpretation and implementation locally. As a result, the non-police forms of policing may differ considerably from city to city and from municipality to municipality.

As was noted in the introductory chapter, international comparison of the police, criminal justice or plural policing may raise many problems of interpretation. In addition to differences in legal rules and formal organization, each country may have its specific unwritten and informal contextual elements, such as the more-or-less implicit meaning of surveillance and enforcement in the public space, long-standing traditions with regard to certain issues, political or emotional sensitivities, or largely hidden interests. Adequate international comparison in this field is only feasible if these differences in cultural, symbolic and emotional context are not ignored (cf. Nelken, 2002).

Despite these limitations and methodological problems, this chapter presents a comparison of plural policing in the five countries studied. Such a comparison must focus on some of the main issues.
The structure of this chapter is as follows. The first question is whether, despite considerable differences between the countries and the strong dependence on the local context, more or less similar patterns and developments can still be found. Are there more or less general factors that have contributed to the pluralization of policing in these countries (7.1)? The focus then transfers to the main differences in plural policing between the countries (7.2). Based upon this analysis of differences and similarities in plural policing, a typology of wardens and enforcement officers is presented (7.3). Finally, the principle of security as a public good is a central concept in the evaluation of the position and work of these non-police wardens and enforcement officers in the public space. In this context four models are presented that may be relevant to understanding future developments in plural policing (7.4). The models are meant to provide food for thought and to fuel debate on the future policy and organization of non-police policing.

7.1 Similarities

Two observations may be made about plural policing in these five countries. Despite fundamental differences between the countries in terms of their police system, government policy, legal conditions, historical, cultural and political contexts, the position and significance of the state and the police, and the relations between local and national (federal) governments, all these countries have witnessed the introduction of new non-police providers of policing in the past few decades. Despite the differences, non-police policing wardens and officers now have an important position in the public space in all these countries. Secondly, despite these great differences, there are important similarities in the processes and circumstances that have contributed to this plural complex of policing. In each of the countries one can observe a similar process, consisting of four main elements.

First, this process starts at the moment the (regular) police fail to meet the predominant expectation that they will be visibly present in the public space, where they will conduct their surveillance tasks, and enforce the norms of social order, social behaviour and decency. The general expectation is that the central tasks of the police should concentrate on social disorder, nuisance, anti-social behaviour, pollution of the public space, and petty crime. The specific factors underlying why the police fail to meet these tasks may differ in each country. Generally, a complex of circumstances and arguments is relevant here, such as a withdrawal of the police (both from the local level and from their presence on the streets), and a shortage of resources to pay sufficient attention to problems of petty crime and other problems that have a negative impact on citizens' feelings of order and security. In some cases this process is prompted by budgetary considerations (police officers may be seen as too expensive compared with wardens or private security officers), the view that the police should concentrate on core tasks, or should spend their resources on tasks with a 'higher' status, such as crime fighting or organized crime. In at least three of the five countries studied, police reform (resulting in an increase in scale and centralization) contributed to this failure of the police. An increasing emphasis on a new managerial discourse may also be relevant (Clarke & Newman, 1997; Pollitt, 1993 and 1998). For the police this may result in a greater emphasis on economy and efficiency (Terpstra & Trommel, 2009).[1]

The second element in the process is that the negative consequences of this development are mainly felt at the local level. Citizens (including shopkeepers and businesspeople) and local governments perceive a serious absence of uniformed surveillance in the public space. It is often assumed that this has a negative impact on citizens' feelings of insecurity and it may undermine their trust in the police. Because these problems mainly arise and are felt at the local level, solutions for the surveillance and enforcement deficit are generally sought at that level.

Thirdly, at the local level these solutions are usually implemented independently of 'normal' police work and (in most cases) outside the regular police force(s). Such measures do not involve an expansion of the regular police force(s) or of the police manpower, but rather the introduction of different, new uniformed workers, like city guards, community guards, wardens, special investigate officers, police community support officers, Ordnungswachen or Stadtwachte (in Austria), parapolice, private security officers with public tasks, by-law enforcers, service guards or surveillance officers (to mention just some examples). The task of these workers and officers involves surveillance in the public space, aimed at

1 In Belgium the process was not primarily promoted by a withdrawal of the police, but by the fact that the public prosecution agency was not able to process the required number of cases.

enhancing feelings of security, social order and the protection of citizens. Some of these officers are also authorized to enforce (local) rules and regulations. As a result, activities that were not long ago defined as regular police work or were even universally seen as the core task of the police, are now (partly) relocated at the margin of the police force or (as happens in most of the countries) even outside the police force. As a result, the once taken-for-granted direct link between the concepts 'police and 'policing' has increasingly been broken (Loader, 2000; Crawford, 2003).

The final element in this process is the rise of a plural policing complex. New public and private forms of surveillance and enforcement in the public space arose alongside the regular police. The notion of one (type of) organization that (in representing the state) has the (claimed) monopoly on policing was gradually abandoned, to be replaced by a plural situation with surveillance and enforcement tasks distributed among a multitude of agencies. In addition, in each country the ways that the new forms of surveillance and enforcement were introduced, are organized and implemented, differ greatly from municipality to municipality. The result is a complexity and diversity in policing, in some cases accompanied by opaqueness and fragmentation.

An important question is how one might understand that, despite greatly divergent contexts such a similar process could arise in all these countries. Four hypotheses seem to be relevant here.
First, it might be assumed that the similar process of pluralization of policing in these countries was the result of comparable police and security policies adopted by national governments. This explanation has only a limited validity. In this field of policy, central governments were often rather reactive, declining to take much initiative. Insofar as there was central government policy, its impact was generally only indirect. Relevant examples here are the (partially unintended) consequences of policies of scale enlargement of police organizations, the growing emphasis on managerial notions and values, and the policy of creating additional employment opportunities for the long-term unemployed (especially in the Netherlands and Belgium). In most cases, however, the current systems of plural policing are not based on an explicit policy plan of a central government, clearly set out in advance;[2] insofar as there was some form of government policy, it was usually an incremental process, created step-by-step (Lindblom, 1979).[3]

2 An exception here may be in England & Wales, where the introduction the PCSOs was based on central government policy.

3 This was clearly the case in Belgium with the processes resulting in the current MAS Act (MAS = Municipal Administrative Sanctions) and the Act on Community Guards.

The second hypothesis might assume that the similarities in the developments of the new surveillance and enforcement professions in the public space are the result of a policy transfer (Newburn & Sparks, 2004). There is convergence in this sort of process because different countries adopt each other's policy concepts, policy notions, organizational models, intervention strategies, or implementation practices, by imitation, deliberate learning, or by the exchange of information and experience, for instance.
To a certain extent, policy transfer was indeed a relevant factor. For example, the introduction of community guards and community guard-recorders in Belgium was inspired by the city guards in the Netherlands. The experience in the Netherlands in the 1990s with city guards and police surveillance officers was also an inspiration in England & Wales to introduce wardens and police community support officers. Later on, the policy transfer moved in the opposite direction: in Belgium and the Netherlands there was a growing interest in the English community support officers, especially in relation to the concept of reassurance policing (Easton et al., 2008).

The third hypothesis might assume that similarities in policing policies and practices are the result of a (common) crisis. Studies on police reform and changes in police policies show that these are often a direct response to crises, such as disasters, scandals, or political incidents (cf. Savage, 2007). Once again, this hypothesis seems to have only a limited relevance to the national policies in this policy domain.[4] Generally, the introduction and growth of these public and private guards and enforcement officers were incremental processes, as the policy, organization and implementation were happening only step-by-step. However, the relevance of this hypothesis may impact especially at the local level, where locally urgent situations or crises were a powerful impetus for local governments to adopt immediately visible measures with a strong symbolic meaning, such as the introduction or expansion of uniformed non-police officers in the public space. However, one might assume that local crises would contribute to differences rather than similarities between the countries.

The fourth hypothesis views the similar rise of non-police officers with surveillance and enforcement tasks in the public space since the early and mid-1990s as the result of parallel social circumstances in these countries: circumstances so significant and unavoidable that they resulted in comparable answers and strategies, despite contextual differences and specific 'drivers' (Savage, 2007) that differed considerably between the countries.

4 An exception may be Canada, where the crisis directly following 9/11 was a powerful impetus for the use of private security officers in the public and semipublic space.

This latter hypothesis is probably the most adequate. In addition to the central government, many public and private actors and agencies have played their roles in this pluralization of policing. Many of the answers to these similar social contexts were created at the local level, often with only a secondary or indirect role for central governments. Policy transfer and political and government crises may also have reinforced certain developments.

Despite the major differences between the countries, there were similarities in the social context that contributed to the process. These factors will only be sketched roughly here. Public safety came to be defined as a significant social problem in all these countries in the 1990s, even if crime and disorder were relatively not serious (as in Austria, for instance). In most countries public safety retained its high political priority even after the level of crime had declined considerably (as has happened in England & Wales and the Netherlands since the beginning of the 21st century) (Millie & Herrington, 2005; Terpstra, 2010a), or if the economic crisis since 2008 meant that other problems became increasingly important and urgent. One of the main responses was the increasingly common political view that more surveillance and enforcement in the public space were necessary and that they legitimated a considerable expenditure of public funds. This also related to significant changes in the urban economy and space, a loss of informal social control, the rise of large-scale events, and the need to regulate behaviour in night-time areas.

At first it was often expected that the police would strengthen their surveillance and enforcement in the public space. Increasingly, however, the police failed to meet these social needs. Because these problems were predominantly felt locally, it was at that level that solutions were often sought. This also reflects other important local developments in many of the countries in those years, such as the introduction of a local integrated security policy and a new distribution of responsibilities in security, with the involvement of many other agencies than the police. The relationships between these elements may differ from country to country, depending for instance on the position of local governments in security policies and the growth and social and political acceptance (cf. White, 2010) of the private security industry.

Finally, in this context an 'opportunity factor' was often also relevant. This created the resources (budgets, manpower) necessary to introduce surveillance and enforcement officers in the public space. For instance, in Belgium and the Netherlands in the 1990s additional employment schemes made it possible for persons living on benefits and the long-term unemployed to be deployed as surveillance officers. All countries studied witnessed a powerful surge in the development of private security. The companies involved attempted to present themselves as pre-eminently suited to fulfilling the growing needs for surveillance and enforcement in the public space. In England & Wales the number of police community support officers could increase thanks to national budgets for neighbourhood policing. Belgium and the Netherlands created new legal instruments, such as systems of (municipal) administrative sanctions, which made it possible for local authorities to engage not only (municipal) surveillance guards or wardens, but also non-police enforcement officers with sanctioning powers.

7.2 Differences

There are also important differences in the ways that these non-police surveillance and enforcement officers were introduced, are organized, and how they operate in the various countries. This analysis concentrates on five main differences.

Privatization

The five countries differ in the extent to which the non-police surveillance and enforcement functions in the public space have been privatized. A distinction may be made between two dimensions; the privatization of providers and the privatization of the auspices (Bayley & Shearing, 2001).

In relation to the privatization of the providers, Belgium is an exceptional case. In contrast to the other countries, Belgium has no private officers who have surveillance and/or enforcement in the public space as their main task. In Belgium a general consensus predominates that these tasks should remain in public hands (although private security companies are trying to get their share of the market). On the other hand, of the countries studied, Canada has the highest level of privatization in policing. In this country an extensive private security industry delivers services in the public and semipublic space, and private agencies and individuals may contract public police officers. Here the distinction between public and private seems to have become fluid. In this context such concepts even seem to have lost much of their traditional meaning.

The three other countries have (different) combinations of public and private. In England & Wales, the Netherlands and Austria, private security officers are working in semipublic places, such as large malls. In England & Wales, as in Canada, private security officers may also be found in business improvement districts. In Austria a significant number of local governments contract private security officers who are charged with surveillance tasks, often in town centres, in some cases also in smaller municipalities. In the Netherlands contracted private security officers may also have some formal legal powers.

The extent to which the auspices are privatized also differs. Once again, in Belgium no surveillance and/or enforcement officers are contracted by private auspices. Canada has the opposite position: private auspices hire all kinds of patrollers and enforcers and even public police officers may be contracted by private agencies. In the other three countries private security officers who are contracted by organizations of shop owners or businesses may be found in (semipublic) malls or industrial estates. In the Netherlands, Canada and England & Wales private security officers are contracted by residents for residential patrol (also in the public space), often in combination with other services, such as alarm monitoring systems, safety checks, and guarding private dwellings (during holidays, for instance, when the residents are away).

Formal regulation

The countries also differ in the extent to which there is specific, formal (legal) regulation of the non-police surveillance and enforcement activities. Belgium has the most clear-cut, elaborate framework for such regulation. The Belgian guards operate on the basis of the Act on Community Guards. In case these community guards also have a so-called recording power, the powers are founded on the MAS (municipal administrative sanctions) Act. Austria and Canada have almost the opposite position. Although Austrian municipalities have the formal duty to enforce local administrative regulations, the non-police municipal city guards have no specific powers.[5] In Canada special constables are appointed by the local police services boards but employed by their own organizations. Mandate and powers are usually defined by agreement with the board. By-law enforcement officers enforce municipal acts; their powers vary from municipality to municipality.

England & Wales and the Netherlands occupy intermediate positions. The community support officers in England & Wales are members of the police forces. This position provides them with the rules and regulations for their work. In the Netherlands there is no specific legal basis for local surveillance officers like the city guards. The tasks and powers of the SIOs (Special Investigative Officers) are defined in a Ministerial Circular. The sanctioning powers of SIOs are laid down in two acts on administrative fines and on government criminal law dispositions. Despite a specific legal system of regulation, local implementation may still be highly divergent and deviate from national rules and policy. For instance in Belgium, with its national legislation on administrative sanctions and community guards, the Flemish part and Wallonia differ strongly in the ways these acts are implemented in practice.

Separation or integration with the police

The five countries also differ in the degree to which there is separation between the wardens and enforcement officers on the one hand, and the police. The greatest contrast here is between Austria and England & Wales.

5 In Austria the regulations differ, for example, between the provinces of Styria and Upper Austria (chapter 4).

In Austria there is a sharp distinction between police work and the responsibilities of the municipal governments (including the Public Order Services and City Guards). This strict separation is a question of legal definition. Apart from this, in practice the police forces and the non-police municipal guards and officers often operate in isolation from each other.

In England & Wales the new surveillance officers are closely integrated, because the community support officers are members of the regular police forces. They also participate in safer neighbourhood teams, together with police officers and (in some cases) wardens or special constables.

The three other countries occupy an intermediate position. The situation in Canada is something of a contradiction. On the one hand there is a close relationship between police officers and parapolice officers (special constables and by-law officers), simply because they are all peace officers and public-sector employees. On the other hand, however, there is quite a distance between these groups and the private security guards who carry out enforcement tasks in public or semipublic space.

In Belgium the division of tasks between the police and the community guard-recorders stems from the legal distinction between different categories of infringements, each with its own MAS procedure. Moreover, in Belgium the police forces and the municipal community guards (with or without specific powers) are legally obliged to co-operate. In practice, relationships between the police and the community guards differ strongly from region to region.

The Netherlands does not have such a strict division between the police and the non-police officers. The Dutch police retain their powers to operate in the domains to which the municipal SIOs are also entitled. Moreover, the police are supposed to do the daily, operational coordination of the SIOs working in the public space. In practice this cooperation often operates rather poorly. The distance between the police and the SIOs is often considerable.

Powers

The formal powers of the non-police professional groups with surveillance and enforcement tasks differ substantially. These differences are not only between countries, but also within each country. In many cases the officers have no formal powers.

In Austria, with the exception of Styria (Graz) and the enforcement of the rules against 'aggressive begging' in Upper Austria (Linz), the municipal city guards do not have specific powers that exceed those of the Everyman's right (*Jedermannsrecht*). This situation is comparable with wardens in England & Wales, city guards in the Netherlands and community guards in Belgium.

In most countries, private security offices working in the public space have no special powers, but there are some exceptions. First there are the private SIOs in the Netherlands, that is, private security officers contracted by municipal governments for enforcement tasks in the public space. They have formal powers, though these are less extensive than those of their colleagues, the public SIOs. In Canada private security officers can be deployed as by-law enforcement officers. In England & Wales private security officers can pass through an accreditation scheme, after which they are entitled to impose a fine.

Matters are different for private security officers who are deployed in a semipublic space (= privately owned, but perceived by citizens as public). They may be able to use the trespass law or the Hausmannsrecht (literally: the right of the man of the house) to deny access or request a visitor to leave the premises.

Some non-police officers who work in the public space have specific formal powers for the enforcement of rules relating to certain infringements. In some cases their sanctioning powers are only indirect, in which case the officers only draw up a report, which may form the basis for a fine imposed by another official. Examples here are the (municipal) SIOs in the Netherlands and the community guard-recorders in Belgium. The Community Support Officers in England & Wales and the special constables and by-law officers in Canada also have specific formal powers.

There are also considerable differences in the powers and means of coercion of the non-police officers, even within individual countries. In some cases there was an explicit intention not to give means of coercion to these non-police officers. It was feared that these non-police officers would become police-like, also in the public's mind, and such a view was usually regarded as inadequate and unattractive. This argument was found in the city of Linz (Austria) in relation to the Public Order Service there, in Belgium (in relation to the community guards (-recorders), and in England & Wales (in relation to the wardens).

In clear contrast, the (public) municipal SIOs in the Netherlands may carry handcuffs, a baton, and pepper spray. This is often legitimated by redefining these means of coercion as providing (self-) protection to the officers. In Austria security guards in public space may have firearms (such as a pistol).

Quality requirements

The five countries also differ considerably in the degree to which there are (formalized) quality requirements for the non-police policing officers. In Austria there are virtually no such requirements. There the organization of the Public Order Services and the recruitment of officers are defined as the responsibility of the municipal government. In Canada there is little adequate regulation of the special constables, with the exception of the province of Alberta.

Some countries have an elaborate system of requirements for the non-police officers, such as England & Wales, the Netherlands and Belgium. The requirements for private security officers (such as a minimum level of education and screening criteria) are usually less strict than those for public officers. Austria has no specific legal regulation of private security. Canada has had such a regulatory system since 2009, but its effectiveness is often viewed as quite poor. In England & Wales such a legal frame-work was instituted in 2001 (White, 2010).

The countries studied differ considerably in each of the five issues. These differences do not relate to each other and are not clearly patterned or structured. Once again, we can see that there is considerable complexity and diversity in the field of plural policing. Moreover, as was noted above, there are not only significant differences between countries, but also within each of them. This is presumably an important reason why it is impossible to discover a clear structure that covers these different aspects of plural policing in the five countries.
This also implies that it is impossible to provide one general explanation for the differences in plural policing. Many factors are relevant here: general views on the position of the state; the dominance of neoliberal discourse and New Public Management and their impact on politics and the public sector; developments in the private security industry (and its regulation); relations between national and local governments; the prevailing police system and its recent changes; relations between local authorities and the police; legal conditions, rules and regulations; political relations and sensitivities, often at several political and governmental levels. There may also be some other relevant, less tangible factors, such as citizens' feelings of insecurity, dissatisfaction with the police and their performance, trust in uniformed officers, the degree to which private security (armed or not) is generally perceived as an accepted and respectable institution, and the extent to which these feelings are translated into political issues and are on the political agenda.
The relevance of these factors for understanding the pluralization of policing in an international context can only be indicated in general terms. To be more specific about the relevance of each of these factors would require a more detailed analysis of differences in regard to separate issues. It can be assumed that such an analysis would show that different combinations of these factors are relevant to understanding national and international differences.

7.3 Types of surveillance and enforcement officers

The preceding chapters have revealed a confusing diversity in contemporary surveillance and enforcement in the (semi-) public space. What is needed is a more precise view of the underlying structure of this diversity. For that purpose a typology is presented of different types of surveillance and enforcement officers in the semipublic space. This typology is an elaboration of a classification published earlier (Terpstra, 2010a), which was based on concepts used by Bayley & Shearing (2001).
The analysis of Bayley and Shearing (2001) had as its starting point that, after a period dominated by the (imagined) monopolization of policing by the police,

now a fundamental restructuring of policing is going on. Originally the authorization of policing and the actual activity of policing lay in the same (governmental) hands. In the view of Bayley and Shearing (2001), in the current process of police restructuring, the functions of authorization and of doing policing became differentiated and separate. This restructuring is even more complex, because in addition to this differentiation there is also privatization, or as Bayley and Shearing (2001: 5) say: 'the auspices and providers of policing become mixed in terms of being public or private'. In other words, with the pluralization of policing over the past two or three decades, both auspices and providers can (independently) be public or private.
The different combinations of public and private gave rise to several types of markets and quasi-markets (LeGrand & Bartlett, 1993) for policing the public space. Each of these (quasi-) markets has its own structure and requires a different form of steering and coordination. One might assume that each of these (quasi-) markets also has its own typical (side-) effects.

In one important respect the analysis presented here differs from that of Bayley & Shearing (2001). They assume that the restructuring of policing implies that both functions will be transferred away from government (2001: vii): 'The contemporary restructuring of policing separates both the authorization of security and the activity of policing from what is recognized as formal government' (p. 5). This argument precedes the theory of Shearing et al. about the nodal governance of security (Johnston & Shearing, 2003; Wood & Shearing, 2007). In that theory the state is seen as only 'one node' among many others. The preceding chapters have shown however that this analysis is not adequate for an understanding of the situation, at least in the continental European countries. The chapters on Austria, Belgium and the Netherlands show that despite processes of pluralization, fragmentation and privatization, the state still occupies a central, unique position (cf. Jones & Newburn, 2002; Crawford, 2003; White & Gill, 2013). Rather than the notion of nodalisation, less radical concepts, such as pluralization or hybridization seem to be more adequate. The relations between public and private (in terms of numbers, complexity, prestige, and dominance) differ from country to country.

A distinction can be made between six types of surveillance and enforcement officers in the public space. These types differ in regard to two elements. The first is whether there is a separation between the authorization of policing and the provider (who carries out the policing activity). Secondly, if there is such a separation, the types differ as to the private and/or public nature of both functions.
In cases where there is no separation between the authorization of policing and the provider, the question that remains is which public agency has the responsibility for both functions. Based on the studies in the five countries we can make

a distinction between the police and the local (municipal) government, which can be the auspice and the provider simultaneously. Table 7.1 presents the six types of surveillance and enforcement officers.

Table 7.1 Six types of non-police surveillance and enforcement officers in (semi-) public space

No separation between auspice and provider		Separation between auspice and provider		
Police	**Local government**		**Public Provider**	**Private Provider**
I	II	Public Auspice	III	IV
		Private Auspice	V	VI

The six types of surveillance and enforcement officers will first be described briefly, with some examples of each type.

Type I No separation between auspice and provider: the police

In the first type there is no separation between the authorization of policing and the provider who does the actual policing. Here the surveillance and enforcement officers are members of the police organization. To a great extent this fits in with the traditional view that the police have the monopoly on policing. However, although these surveillance and enforcement officers are members of the police force, they are not full police officers. Because of their limited tasks and powers these auxiliary officers are often seen as having a lower social status (both in the police organization and the outside world), although the officers are charged with a core element of the police mandate, i.e. the visible presence in the public space and keeping up relations with citizens (Terpstra, 2012a).

Some examples of this type of policing officer are the police surveillance officers in the Netherlands and the community support officers in England & Wales. Both are members of the regular police organization and have formal powers, but these are less extensive than those of 'normal' police officers. Although the community support officers wear a police-like uniform, it is easy for citizens to see that they are not regular police officers. Nevertheless, many citizens are very satisfied with their presence and performance (see chapter 3).

Type II No separation between auspice and provider: municipal government

The second type of surveillance and enforcement also has no separation between the authorization and the provider. Here both functions are placed with the city or municipal government.

In the present study this type was encountered more often than type 1. The Belgian community guards (with and without recording powers) are examples. This category also includes the municipal Public Order Services and City Guard Departments in Austria, and the City Guards and SIOs working in the public space in the Netherlands. In these three countries one notices a growing distance between the local governments and the police. Local governments have tried to create answers to the negative consequences of this growing distance by establishing their own surveillance and enforcement schemes and by introducing municipal (non-police) officers with policing tasks in the public space. The wardens in England & Wales and the by-law enforcement officers in Canada can also be included in this category.

Type III Public agencies purchasing public surveillance/enforcement capacities

In this case the authorization and provider of policing are separate. A public agency purchases surveillance or enforcement capacity from another public organization.

This situation can be found for instance in Canada (Ontario). Here the purchase of policing is a regular way to organize police services (so-called contract policing). If local governments do not have their own police force, they can purchase police capacity from the Ontario Provincial Police. The local government may decide to select another provider after the contract expires.[6] Several contracted police forces may be operative within the territory of a single municipality.

A somewhat comparable situation may be found in the Netherlands, although it is not very common. In the early 2000s rural municipalities in the province of Utrecht were faced with a withdrawal of the police from their villages. The local governments tried to create an alternative by contracting police surveillance officers and in some cases community police officers with the regional police force (Terpstra, 2004). These community police officers have full police powers. The surveillance police officers in the Netherlands (just like the Canadian special constables who are contracted by hospitals and universities), are auxiliary officers, employed in the police force, not having full powers.

Type IV Private security contracted by public agencies

Government agencies can also purchase private security officers as wardens, guards or enforcement officers in the public space. This form of contracting may be found in the Business Improvement Districts of the inner cities in Canada and in England & Wales. Here private security officers may work in public-private partnerships, with the local government as one of the funding agencies. In other cases a public agency may be the authorizer of this form of policing, for instance in Toronto (Canada) where (public) housing corporations contract private secur-

6 A comparable form of contracting may be found in a small number of cases in England & Wales (Crawford & Lister, 2006).

ity officers. In Austria a considerable number of local governments, mainly in medium-sized cities, contract private security officers to work in the public space. These officers have no specific police powers.
In the Netherlands local governments may contract private security officers as SIOs in the public space. These SIO's have fewer formal powers than public SIOs. In Canada private security officers may be contracted as bylaw enforcement officers. In England & Wales private security officers may have enforcement powers if they have followed an accreditation scheme. Local governments have rarely used this option at the time of writing.

Type V Private agencies purchasing public officers

In this case public officers are contracted by private agencies. This was found most frequently in Canada. Here it is not unusual for paid duty officers (who are sworn police officers) to be contracted by private agencies. This can be arranged at both the individual level (with the police officer moonlighting in addition to regular police work), and at the collective level. In the latter case the purchaser has a contract with the police force with police officers performing activities for the purchaser in addition to their regular police duty hours. In Canada large malls and Business Improvement Districts may contract paid duty officers, for instance to patrol. This is to some extent comparable to the situation in England & Wales, where the management of shopping malls may hire police officers (sometimes called 'village bobbies').
In the Netherlands this happens only as an exception. Van Steden (2007) mentions a large mall in the city of Utrecht, which is patrolled by public officers contracted by private agencies. In this country there is occasional public debate about the question whether the public police should not be paid for their services during professional football matches and other large-scale commercial events. So far this has not been put into practice.

Type VI Private providers contracted by private auspices

Finally, private guards and surveillance officers are contracted by private auspices. Apart from the private space, in most cases these officers are working in the semipublic space, like large private properties, business parks, industrial estates or large malls.
There are also examples of private security officers who are contracted by private auspices to patrol in and guard the public space. This may happen in the direct vicinity of large industrial estates, where private security guards also patrol the nearby public roads. Especially in high-income neighbourhoods (unions of) residents may contract private security officers for residential patrol, including the public space, in combination with other services like alarm monitoring. This can be found (to varying degrees) in Canada, England & Wales, Austria, and the

Netherlands. In England & Wales private security officers may also be contracted by private agencies to manage anti-social behaviour.

These different types of surveillance and enforcement officers show that non-police forms of contemporary policing have a very complex, very divergent structure. This is all the more so because the different types may be combined in practice. For instance, in Business Improvement Districts the authorizing agencies can be public, private or public-private. The same applies to the providers of policing in these districts.

The typology can also be used to show the differences between the countries. Table 7.2 gives an indication of the relative importance of the various types of surveillance and enforcement officers in each of the countries.

Table 7.2 Six types of surveillance and enforcement officers in the public and semipublic space in five countries

	No separation auspice-provider		Separation auspice-provider			
	Police I	Local government II	Public – public III	Public – private IV	Private – public V	Private – private VI
The Netherlands		+++		+		+
England & Wales	+++	+		+	+	+
Austria		+++		+		+
Belgium		+++				
Canada – Ontario		+	+	+++	++	+

Table 7.2 shows a considerable diversity in the types of surveillance and enforcement officers found in the public space in most of the countries studied. In this respect Belgium is an important exception. In Belgium the private security industry does not have an important position in the public space.
The surveillance and enforcement functions in England & Wales and Canada are far more complex, partly because the private security industry has a prominent position in these countries. The Netherlands and Austria occupy an intermediate position.

7.4 Security as a public good: four models

Despite considerable differences between the countries, there are also significant similarities in the development and position of the non-police policing officers.

What the countries have in common is that policing can no longer be imagined or claimed to be the exclusive task of the police. Other agencies than the police have gained important positions in policing and security. With the exception of Belgium, private security now plays an important role in the public space. In addition to the traditional coordination by (local) governments, coordination by (quasi-) market processes has become more prominent. These developments resulted in a very complex, diverse and often opaque situation, which raises important questions. What are the consequences of this pluralization of policing for the way citizens are treated in the public space? How are citizens' rights protected and what guarantees do citizens have in their relations with guards, wardens, surveillance workers and enforcement officers? What are the main priorities for these non-police officers, who decides on these priorities, and which interests play a role? How are the activities and actors of plural policing coordinated? What does the presence of all these wardens, guards and enforcement officers mean for public safety, feelings of security, citizens' trust in the police and in government? To what extent do these non-police policing officers reassure citizens, or does their uniformed presence increase risk awareness (Zedner, 2003)? Do these non-police policing officers contribute to social exclusion and decreasing accessibility of the public space? Is the growth of non-police policing an indication of the growth of a control society (Van Waarden, 2006) or a surveillance society (Lyon, 2001)?

Many of these questions are also relevant with respect to future developments in the field. Will the growth and diversification of these non-police officers continue? To what extent will the withdrawal by the police from local surveillance and enforcement continue? Will local governments still feel the need and have the resources to create their own local policing force, as has happened in several countries in recent years? What consequences will this have for the regular police: will they concentrate even more on national priorities and crime fighting? Given the growth of private security, will this industry acquire even more tasks and powers and what will this mean for public-private relations in policing and security? What consequences may this have for the accessibility of urban space, social exclusion, the social distribution of security, and the position and treatment of citizens? How can one regulate and supervise these new forms of policing in more democratic and transparent ways?

These questions often relate to important norms and values. In their consequences they may be far more fundamental than the managerial issues that often dominate policy agendas in this field, such as the problems of economy, effectiveness and efficiency, and how to reduce overlaps between different providers. These social values relate to important issues like justice, equality, fair treatment, protection of citizens, safeguards against non-legitimate forms of coercion, legal certainty, equity, and proportionality. The underlying values of security and

policing may also touch on notions of solidarity, social trust and civilization (Terpstra, 2010a).
The values underlying policing and security may be contradictory. For instance, the needs of security may conflict with liberty (Bauman, 2001). These values may also be opposite in their effects. More surveillance and a strict style of enforcement may contribute to feelings of security and protection, but may also raise risk awareness and undermine social trust and solidarity. The search for security for one group of persons may be detrimental to the liberty of others.

These normative questions relate to different aspects of security as a public good (Loader & Walker, 2007). The central question is how this public good can be achieved in conditions of plural policing. This complex question cannot be answered unequivocally, not only because plural policing is highly complex and differentiated, but also because policing and security refer to opposing values and entail several substantial paradoxes. In other words, policing and security are not only a public, but also an unqualified good (Zedner, 2003).

A complete, detailed answer to these important questions is not feasible here, so another approach has been adopted. Several models are distinguished that point to different potential future trajectories in plural policing. These models mainly concern the relations between public and private and the governance of multi-agency networks of policing. This refers not only to managerial issues (such as efficiency and cost reduction), but also to citizens' rights and other fundamental values underlying security and policing.
These four models are inspired by the different patterns and developments of plural policing in the countries studied, the problems raised there, the strategies used to cope with these problems, and the various public debates on plural policing. The treatment of the models is confined to some of the main issues. Some potential positive (strong) elements and potential risks (weaknesses) are distinguished for each model. In describing these elements, the inherent logic and assumptions of each model is followed as far as possible. The models are presented in a general way, without further reference to individual countries. The recognisability of the models may differ from country to country. However, the models may be relevant to imagining potential future developments in plural policing and to promoting public debate on public and private in policing.

I. Integration in the police

The main assumption of the first model is that the rise of non-police providers of policing is to be regretted (see Fijnaut, 2012). This development has resulted in considerable complexity and fragmentation, making high demands on coordination and governance. The complexity and fragmentation and the problems of coordination may imply that the system of plural policing will fail to meet the standards of security as a public good. In this view such problems can only be solved by (re-) defining surveillance and enforcement in the public space as proper police tasks. Policing should go back to the police and must be performed only by fully fledged police officers. There is no place for private security officers in the public space. By (once again) making policing a public institution there is more room for effective democratic control and accountability. Two central considerations are that the police have a monopoly of coercive means and have relevant expertise and experience. Integrating surveillance and enforcement tasks in the police organization will make the coordination of policing less problematic. This model assumes that by bringing 'back' non-police forms of policing into the police force, the symbolic capital and traditional authority of the police can also be beneficial for the performance and social acceptability of these other policing activities. In conclusion, the dispersal of policing across several public and private agencies should be terminated.

Table 7.3 Integration in the police

Strengths	Potential risks
• surveillance and enforcement in public space remain acknowledged as public police tasks • surveillance and enforcement in public space performed by full and professional police officers • surveillance and enforcement can be based upon the authority and legitimacy of the police • means of coercion in the hands of one agency • fewer problems of coordination	• surveillance and enforcement in the public space will still depend on the willingness and resources of the police to perform these local tasks • surveillance and enforcement in the public space may depend on other police priorities with a 'higher' status • local surveillance and enforcement in the public space may depend on national or central policy priorities • the risk that surveillance and enforcement in the public space may result in repressive styles of policing (the problem of 'mowing grass on Sunday') • distance to local government and policy • other actors may retreat (from now on, it is generally considered to be the responsibility of the police alone) • declining opportunities for a holistic, multi-agency approach

II. Police as the coordinator

The second model accepts the rise and existence of the non-police providers of policing as a given. To a certain extent the distribution of tasks and responsibilities over a multitude of agencies is appreciated. It creates room for a holistic approach to problems of crime, disorder and feelings of insecurity. The main principle of this model is that the police should occupy the central position in the plural policing complex. The arguments are comparable with those underlying the first model: the police are seen as well-equipped for such a role, because of their authority, expertise, specific means and powers. Because of the central position of the police in policing and security, this model will deliver fewer problems of coordination.

The central role of the police can be found in two different forms. First, the surveillance and enforcement officers may be members of the police organization, without becoming full police officers. This is the position of the PCSOs in England & Wales. It was the original reason for introducing police surveillance officers in the Netherlands. Secondly, the police can be the coordinator of the (public and private) non-police providers of policing. This model can be found in the English Crime and Disorder Reduction Partnerships. Because surveillance and enforcement in the public space are largely local phenomena, this model assumes that the police have a strong local position. The current trend in many Northern and Western European countries is to centralize or nationalize police forces. One risk of such a restructuring may be an erosion of the local position of the police (Fyfe, Terpstra & Tops, 2013).

Table 7.4 Police as the coordinator

Strengths	Potential risks
• multi-agency approach to policing and security • more room for a local, integrated policy on public safety • coordination of the plural policing can use the social authority, legitimacy and expertise of the police • direct relation between the coordination of policing and the (public) police • the coordination can create a more direct relation between (regular) police work and the (non-police) providers of policing	• coordination is (partly) not in the hands of the authorizer and funder of non-police providers of policing • no direct relation between the coordination of plural policing and the local, integrated public safety policy (of the local government) • coordination may depend on interests and views of the police • coordination may be seen as a marginal task because it does not belong to the 'police core business' or 'real police work' • coordination may pay more attention to repression and crime fighting than to prevention, police visibility, reassurance and other local policing activities • tension between police as a coordinator with a wide-ranging role and the need for the police as specialists • a certain level of fragmentation • in countries with a trend towards centralization of the police: the risk of erosion of the local position of the police

III. Local government as the coordinator

The third model also assumes a distribution of surveillance and enforcement tasks in the public space over a large number of (public and private) agencies. Here it is not the police but the local government that occupies the central position. Two main arguments are relevant here. First, the police lost too much credibility by withdrawing from the local level or by neglecting essential tasks of surveillance and enforcement in the public space. By doing so, the police left serious gaps for other agencies to fill. Secondly, the local (municipal) governments should play this role, because they are best suited to coordinate the broad, multi-agency field of local security. In countries like the Netherlands, Belgium and Austria the local governments are increasingly the central agency in and coordinator of local integrated public safety policy. From this perspective it seems evident that local governments should also occupy such a position in (local) plural policing. This will promote coordination between plural policing and local public safety policy. In addition, with this position local authorities acquire the means to be an 'armed local government', a popular concept among some local politicians in the Netherlands and the Flemish part of Belgium. By having their own municipal enforcement guards with sanctioning powers, local governments can use coercive means in the management of social disorder and (petty) crime, without depending on the police. In this model the non-police policing officers and the local authorities are in a direct relationship. There is also more room for local democratic control and accountability. Significant developments in Belgium, Austria and the Netherlands fit with this model.

Table 7.5 Local government as the central actor

Strengths	Potential risks
• direct link with (coordination of) local public safety policy • direct relation with funding and policy responsibilities • authorizer and provider partially not separated (municipal guards and officers) • no dependence on withdrawing police and/or other police priorities and views • creating the means for an 'armed local government' • more room for local democratic control and accountability	• at distance from the public police • creating a potential excuse for the police for even further withdrawal from local surveillance and enforcement tasks • fragmentation and great differentiation in policing may continue • dependence on local political incidents and hypes • the culture of local governments may be more policy-oriented than focused on practical and urgent matters (whereas the opposite may be required) • coordination by local government may be hampered by internal fragmentation (Terpstra, 2008)

IV. Marketization

According to this model a transfer of tasks and responsibilities in policing to the market would provide opportunities to avoid top-down government steering, with all its limitations and negative consequences. In this view there is no valid reason why the public police should occupy a more prominent position than other agencies in policing, including private agencies and commercial companies. The police organization is viewed as clumsy, taking too much taxpayers' money. Although in this view the state may still have a regulatory function, the market is seen as competent to arrange the coordination of surveillance and enforcement tasks, also in the public space. Local surveillance, control and patrol may be left to free-market organizations. Criminal law enforcement and 'high policing' are seen as the only tasks that should remain a monopoly of the public police. To a certain degree this model corresponds with the theory of the nodal governance of security (Wood & Shearing, 2007), mentioned previously. The current situation in the continental European countries differs greatly from this model. However, plural policing in Canada does bear some similarities with this model.

Table 7.6 Marketization

Strengths	Potential risks
• the promise of the 3 E's • flexibility, tailor-made solutions, 'client oriented' • police can focus on core tasks (*crime fighting*) • the actual policing is not dependent on state bureaucracies (separation between 'steering' and 'rowing' (Osborne & Gaebler, 1992) • authorization distributed over several public and private agencies • emphasis on prevention and risk management	• fragmentation • problems of governance (problems of principal-agency relations) • economic considerations and the interests of private security companies may have an impact on the surveillance and enforcement in the public space • means of coercion also in the hands of private agencies • problems of democratic control and public accountability • limitations on the free accessibility of public space and exclusion of weak or 'undesired' citizens • police may concentrate on core tasks, be reduced in manpower; as a result the police will be at a greater distance from the general public; negative consequences for legitimacy and citizens' trust • unequal distribution of (the benefits of) policing and security

The four models refer to different future trajectories in plural policing. The pluralization of policing was frequently not based on clear visions of the future of surveillance and enforcement in the public space, nor on explicit considerations of how policing and security could be organized to meet the standards of a public good. In the main, short-term considerations and ad hoc interests were decisive. Because policing and security are strongly related to important social values, more explicit views and well-founded arguments are needed to direct future developments in this field. Public debates should be started about the future of policing, the relations between public and private agencies and interests in this field, and the importance of policing as a public good.

The four potential trajectories represented by these models may be used to structure thinking about the future of policing and security and about the negative and positive consequences that may arise from policy decisions. These models only give a first, provisional impression of the consequences of certain policy choices. The central question is: what kind of policing do we want? Do we want a police that concentrates on its core (business) tasks, a sort of minimal policing, defined as highly sophisticated and technology-driven, concentrating on national priorities, operating in isolation from citizens and local communities, defining surveillance and enforcement of social disorder and petty crime as inefficient, not real police work, or as only the final item on the list? Or do we want a police force that sees a visible and approachable presence for citizens as its main task, its position in local communities as an essential element of the work, and the surveillance and enforcement of disorder and petty crime as a main starting point for many of the other activities? The answers to these rather general, but fundamental questions have direct implications for the organization of policing in the public space and for the question whether (and if so, how) non-police providers of policing should be used in addition to the regular police.

Other important questions have to do with the integration of policing: to what extent is a differentiation of policing in different kinds or organizations desirable? How should the relations be between public and private in policing, in responsibilities, powers and in regulation? In many countries the pluralization of policing depends closely on the relations between national and local levels, both in government structures and in the organization of the police. How autonomous are local governments and to what extent should they be held responsible for finding solutions for problems in local policing created at higher levels of government? A related question (one that is highly relevant in some of the countries, but not in others) is whether policing of local rules and regulations should be treated as proper police work, or as the responsibility of the local administration. In the latter case local governments may feel the need to create their own non-police policing agencies, independent of the regular police, and often with fewer powers.

Three other questions are also important here. The first has to do with the coordination and regulation of non-police policing activities. The coordination may refer to different aspects: general governmental policy, regulation by means of quality requirements, and the (operational) coordination of the policing work at the street level. Which agency should be responsible for coordination and regulation and how should they be done? Secondly, an important issue concerns the formal powers of non-police surveillance and enforcement officers. What powers should they have, under what conditions, how should citizens' rights be protected against the use or abuse of such powers, how can citizens resist abuse or complain about the non-police officers? Thirdly, how should democratic control and accountability of the non-police policing agencies and officers be advanced? How can one prevent policing from becoming highly dependent on local political incidentalism, hypes and power relations, and how can we prevent it becoming dependent on populist movements to exclude 'unwanted' citizens?

Despite significant international differences in plural policing, for the past few decades the countries studied here have been faced with similar problems: the failure of the police to meet the expectation that they will deliver essential policing activities at the local level; local governments and other local agencies trying to create alternatives for the regular police, resulting in complex and often fragmented systems of plural policing. What is remarkable is that in this process national governments often only make a minor, indirect contribution. The resulting pluralization of policing, a phenomenon that is especially significant at the local level, is a very incremental process, with many different public and private agencies involved. It is also a risky process, because policing is related to central social and public values. The awareness of these risks often seems to be quite minimal.

Without a clear vision of the future of (plural) policing, one might expect that in the near future the marketization model will become more prominent. In the short run this may seem like an adequate solution. In an age of austerity, it might be attractive to decrease the demands made on the state and the police. However, in the long run it may be a highly risky strategy, not only for the nature of policing and security as public goods, but also for the legitimacy of the police and the state and for citizens' trust in these core institutions. Governments, and the police especially, cannot neglect essential tasks like policing local social disorder and petty crime without creating their own self-defeating processes. This cannot be compensated by an opaque patchwork of private and local agencies, which are considered to fill the gaps left by the police.

Appendix

List of interviewed persons[1]

Engeland & Wales

John Chadwick – Crime & Anti Social Behaviour Reduction Unit, Home Office, London.

John DeSousa – Special Constables, Home Office, London.

Kate Lloyd – Local & Neighbourhood Policing Unit, Home Office, London.

Barry Loveday – Reader, Institute of Criminal Justice, University of Portsmouth.

Peter Neyroud – Former Chief Constable of Thames Valley Police and chief executive officer for the National Policing Improvement Agency; visiting professor, University of Chester.

Betsy Stanko – Deputy head of Strategy and Performance, London Metropolitan Police.

Alison Wakefield – Senior lecturer in Security and Risk Management, Institute of Criminal Justice, University of Portsmouth.

Austria

Michael Danzinger – Director, City Management Mödling GmbH, Mödling.

Walter Fuchs – Researcher, Institute for the sociology of law and criminology (IRKS), Vienna.

---

1 The sequence in this list of interviewed persons does not correspond with the numbers of the interviewees used in the previous chapters.

Karl-Heinz Grundböck – Chairman, Federal Ministry of the Interior, Vienna.

Rainhard Kriechbaum – Director Department of Order, municipality of Linz.

Manfred Sulzer – Chief Inspector, Police, Mödling.

Gregor Wenda – Deputy Director Department of Elections, Federal Ministry of the Interior, Vienna; deputy chief editor Öffentliche Sicherheit.

Belgium

Rebecca Boi – Director, Judicial Department and Knowledge Management, the City of Ghent.

Marc Cools – Professor of Criminology, Ghent University and Free University of Brussels.

Kim Geenens – Unit manager, Department of community guards – community guards-recorders, The City of Ghent.

Tom Meeuws – Staff member Prevention Policy and director of SamenLeven, The City of Antwerp.

Rachel Vanderhaegen – Staff member Prevention Policy, The Municipality of Evere (Brussel).

Philip Willekens – Acting director-general, Directorate-General for Security and Prevention Policy, Federal Public Service Interior, Brussels

Canada – Ontario

Glenn de Caire – Chief of the Hamilton Police Service, Hamilton.

Ted Carroll – President of Policing & Security Management Services Inc., Mississauga.

Dan Hutt – Director, Campus Police Services, University of Toronto Campus Community Police Service, Toronto.

George Rigakos – Professor of the Political Economy of Policing, Department of Law and Legal Studies, Carleton University, Ottawa.

Brian Robertson – Consultant Security Training Expert, Legal and Regulatory Compliance, David Hyde & Associates, Toronto.

Leo Russomanno – Lawyer, Webber Schroeder Goldstein Abergel, Criminal Lawyers Ottawa.

References

ACPO (Association of Chief Police Officers of England, Wales & Northern Ireland) (2007). *Guidance of Police Community Support Officers*, London: ACPO.

Barker, A. and Crawford, A. (2013). 'Policing urban insecurities through visible patrols: Managing public expectations in times of fiscal restraint', in: R. Lippert and K. Walby (eds.), *Policing cities: Urban Securitization and Regulation in a 21st Century World,* London: Routledge.

Bayley, D. and Shearing, C. (2001). *The New Structure of Policing: Description, Conceptualization, and Research Agenda*, Washington D.C.: National Institute of justice.

Belser, I. de (2012). *De GAS-wetgeving in de strijd tegen overlast,* Gent: Universiteit Gent, Faculteit der Rechtsgeleerdheid (master's thesis).

Berghuis, A. and Waard, J. de (2012). 'De valkuilen van de probleemgerichte politiezorg', *Justitiële Verkenningen*, 38 (5): 50-62.

Bittner, E. (1970). *The Functions of the Police in Modern Society. A review of background factors, current practices, and possible role models*, Cambridge (Mass.): Oelgeschlager, Gunn & Hain.

Brown, J. and Lippert, R. (2007). 'Private Security's Purchase: Imaginings of a Security Patrol in a Canadian Residential Neighbourhood', *Canadian Journal of Criminology and Criminal Justice*, 49 (5): 587-616.

Bruggeman, W., Devroe, E. and Easton, M. (eds.) (2010). *Evaluatie van 10 jaar politiehervorming: Terugkijken in het verleden en vooruitkijken in de toekomst*, Antwerpen: Maklu Uitgevers.

Burbidge, S. (2005). 'The Governance Deficit: Reflections on the Future of Public and Private Policing in Canada', *Canadian Journal of Criminology and Criminal Justice*, 47 (1): 63-86.

Button, M. (2007). 'Assessing the Regulation of Private Security across Europe', *European Journal of Criminology*, 4 (1): 109–128.

Carroll, E. (2004a). *A Report on University Campus Policing and Security in Canada,* Ottawa: Law Commission of Canada (Background paper prepared for the Law Commission of Canada).

Carroll, E. (2004b). *The Blurring of Public Police and Private Agencies*, Mississauga: Policing & Security Consulting Services.

Clarke J. and Newman, J. (1997). *The Managerial State: Power, politics and ideology in the making of new welfare,* London: Sage Publications Limited.

CoESS (2011). *Private Security Services in Europe. Facts & Figures 2011*, Wemmel: CoESS.

Cook, I. (2010). 'Policing, Partnerships, and Profits: The Operations of Business Improvement Districts and Town Centre Management Schemes in England', *Urban Geography*, 31(4): 453-478.

Cools, M. and Verbeiren, K. (2008). 'De private en bijzondere veiligheid in de publieke ruimte: een wettelijke kijk', in: P. Ponsaers, and E. Devroe (eds.), *Publieke ruimte, Cahiers integraal veiligheidsbeleid, Politeia*, pp. 39-52.

Cooper, C. et al. (2006). *A national evaluation of Community Support Officers*, London: Home Office.

Cops, D., Put, J. and Pleysier, S. (2012). 'De GAS-wetgeving als instrument voor de aanpak van overlast. Bedenkingen bij en suggesties voor een integraal en onderbouwd overlastbeleid', *Panopticon*, 33(6): 552-563.

Coward, S., Etherington, D., Macmillan, R. and Wells, P. (2004). *Neighbourhood wardens: More than the 'Eyes and Ears' of Communities?*, Sheffield: Sheffield Hallam University.

Crawford, A. (2003). 'Contractual Governance of Deviant Behaviour', *Journal of Law and Society*, 30(4): 479-505.

Crawford, A. (2006a). 'Policing and security as 'club goods': the new enclosures?', in: J. Wood and B. Dupont (eds.), *Democracy, Society and the Governance of Security*, Cambridge: Cambridge University Press: pp. 111-138.

Crawford, A., (2006b). "Fixing Broken Promises?': Neighbourhood Wardens and Social Capital', *Urban Studies*, 43 (5/6): 957-976.

Crawford, A. (2007). 'Crime prevention and community safety', in: M. Maguire, R. Morgan and R. Reiner (eds.), *The Oxford Handbook of Criminology* (fourth edition), Oxford: Oxford University Press: pp. 866-909.

Crawford, A. (2008). 'Plural policing in the UK: policing beyond the police', in: T. Newburn (ed.), *The Handbook of Policing* (second edition), Devon: Willan Publishing: pp. 147-181.

Crawford, A. (2011). 'From the shopping mall to the street corner: dynamics of exclusion in the governance of public space', in: A. Crawford (eds.), *International and Comparative Criminal Justice and Urban Governance. Convergence and Divergence in Global, National and Local Settings*, Cambridge University Press: pp. 483-518.

Crawford, A., Blackburn, S., Lister, S. and Shepherd, P. (2005). *Patrolling with a Purpose: an Evaluation of Police Community Support Officers in Leeds and Bradford City Centres*, Leeds: CCJS Press.

Crawford, A. and Lister, S. (2003). 'The patchwork shape of reassurance policing in England and Wales', *Policing*, 27(3): 413-430.

Crawford, A. and Lister, S. (2004). *The extended policing family: Visible patrols in residential areas*, Joseph Rowntree Foundation/University of Leeds.

Crawford, A., Lister, S., Blackburn, S. and Burnett, J. (2005). *Plural Policing: The Mixed Economy of Visible Patrols in England and Wales*, Bristol: Policy Press.

Crawford, A. and Lister, S. (2006). 'Additional Security Patrols in Residential Areas: Notes from the Marketplace', *Policing and Society*, 16(2): 164-188.

Crijns, J. (2010). 'Een terugtocht van de politie uit de openbare ruimte? Over consequenties van de bestuurlijke strafbeschikking en de bestuurlijke boete overlast in de openbare ruimte voor de taak en de positie van de politie', *Strafblad*, 5: 371-386.

Cukier, W., Quigley, T. and Susla, J. (2003). 'Canadian regulation of private security in an international perspective', *International Journal of the Sociology of Law*, 31: 239-265.

Davey, H. (2010). *Safer Neighbourhoods Scrutiny*, London: Metropolitan Police Authority.

Devroe, E. (2012). 'A swelling culture of control? – De genese en toepassing van de wet op de gemeentelijke administratieve sancties in België', Antwerpen: Maklu (diss.).

Devroe, E. and Ponsaers, P. (2011). 'Bestuurlijke aanpak van kleine ordeverstoringen in drie Europese landen', in: B. van Stokkom, J. Terpstra, M. Easton (eds.), *Social Disorder, Cahier Politiestudies*, 2011-1: 221-246.

Donnelly, D. (2013). *Municipal Policing in the European Union: Comparative Perspectives*, Houndmills: Palgrave Macmillan.

Downes, D. and Van Swaaningen, R. (2007). 'The road to dystopia? Changes in the penal climate of the Netherlands', *in: M.* Tonry and C. Bijleveld (eds.), *Crime and justice in the Netherlands*, Chicago: Chicago University Press: pp. 31-71.

Easton, M., Gunther Moor, L., Hoogenboom, B., Ponsaers, P. and Stokkom, B. van (eds.) (2008). *Reflections on Reassurance Policing in the Low Countries*, Den Haag: Boom Juridische uitgevers.

Enhus, E., Verwee, I., Altert, K. van, Verhage, A. and Hoste, J. (2005). *De nieuwe functies inzake veiligheid. Eindrapport werkingsjaar 2005*, Brussel: FOD Binnenlandse Zaken.

Elzinga, D. (2007). 'Het politiebestel', in: Fijnaut, C. et al. (eds.), *Politie. Studies over haar werking en organisatie*, Deventer: Kluwer: pp. 87-107.

Fijnaut, C. (2012). *Het Nationale Politiekorps*, Amsterdam: Uitgeverij Bert Bakker.

Flight, S., Hartmann, A., and Nauta, O. (2012). *Bestuurlijke strafbeschikking en bestuurlijke boete overlast. Evaluatie na drie jaar*, Den Haag: WODC.

Foster, J. and Jones, C. (2010). '"Nice to do" and Essential: Improving Neighbourhood Policing in an English Police Force', *Policing*, 4(4): 395-402.

Fuchs, W. (2005). *Private Sicherheitsdienste und öffentlicher Raum. Ein Überblick über die öffentlichen-rechtlichen Rahmenbedingungen in Österreich mit rechtstatsächlichen und kriminologischen Anmerkungen*, Innsbruck: Universität Innsbruck (diss.).

Fuchs, W. (2012). 'Sicherheit als faszinierendes Geschäftsvehikel? Zur Effektivität kommerzieller und staatlicher Sicherheitsarbeit', *SIAK-Journal. Zeitschrift für Polizeiwissenschaft und polizeilicher Praxis*, 1: 62-75.

Fyfe, N., Terpstra J. and Tops, P. (eds.) (2013) *Centralizing Forces? Comparative perspectives on contemporary police reform in Northern and Western Europe*, Den Haag: Boom/Eleven.

Garland, D. (2001). *The culture of control: Crime and social order in contemporary society*, Oxford: Oxford University Press.

Giddens, A. (1991). *Modernity and Self-Identity: Self and Society in the Late Modern Age*, Stanford: Stanford University Press.

Girling, E., Loader, I. and Sparks, R. (2000). *Crime and Social Change in Middle England: Questions of Order in an English Town*, London: Routledge.

Haagsma, J., Rümke, T., Smits, I., Veer, E. van der and Wiebrens, C. (2012). *De Sterkte van de Arm: feiten en mythes*, Apeldoorn: Politie & Wetenschap.

Haagsma, J.H., I. Smits, H. Waarsing & C.J. Wiebrens (2012). *Blauw, hier en daar. Onderzoek naar de sterkte van de politie in Nederland, België, Denemarken, Engeland & Wales en Nordrhein-Westfalen*, Apeldoorn: Politie & Wetenschap, 2012.

Hauber, A. Dijk, B. van, Hofstra, L., Loef C., Molen, F. van der, Toornvliet, L. and Zandbergen, J. (1994). *Stadswachten: Effectiviteit, draagvlak en organisatorische aspecten*, Den Haag: Ministerie van Justitie, Stafafdeling Informatievoorziening, Directie Criminaliteitspreventie.

Hemmer, D. and Bauer, W. (2003). *Privatisierung und Liberalisierung öffentlicher Dienstleistungen in der EU-15: Sicherheit*, Wien: Österreichische Gesellschaft für Politikberatung und Politikentwicklung.

Hennekens, H. (2011). 'Het wetsvoorstel voor een nationale politie', *De gemeentestem*, 99, 161/7360: 521-534.

Hermer, J., Kempa, M., Shearing, C., Stenning, P. and Wood, J. (2005). 'Policing in Canada in the Twenty-first Century: Directions for Law Reform' in: D. Cooley (eds.), *Re-imagining Policing in Canada*, Toronto: University of Toronto Press.

HMIC (2010), *Valuing the Police: Policing in austerity*, (www.hmic.gov.uk/media/valuing-the-police-policing-in-an-age-of-austerity-20100720.pdf, retrieved at 9 October 2012).

HMIC (2012), *Policing in austerity: One year on*, (www.hmic.gov.uk/media/policing-in-austerity-one-year-on.pdf, retrieved at 9 October 2012).

Home Office (2004). *Building Communities, Beating Crime: A Better Police Service for the 21st Century*, Cm 6360, London.

Home Office (2011). *Police and crime commissioners, have you got what it takes?*, London.

Home Office (2012). *Statistical Bulletin 03/12* (www.homeoffice.gov.uk/publications/science-research-statistics/research-statistics/police-research/hosb1311/hosb1311?view=Binary, retrieved at 9 October 2012).

Hoogenboom, A. (1994). *Het politiecomplex. Over de samenwerking tussen politie, bijzondere opsporingsdiensten en particuliere recherche*, Arnhem: Gouda Quint.

Hope, T. (2005). 'The new local governance of community safety in England & Wales', *Canadian Journal of Criminology and Criminal Justice*, 47(2): 369-387.

Huberts, L. et al. (2004). *Paradoxaal politiebestel. Burgemeesters, Openbaar Ministerie en Politiechefs over de sturing van de politie*, Zeist: Kerckebosch/Politie & Wetenschap.

Hughes, G. (2004). 'Besturen via misdaad en geweld? Publiek-private samenwerking bij de aanpak van criminaliteit en geweld in Engeland en Wales', *Justitiële verkenningen*, 30(7): 24-40.

Huey, L., Ericson, R. and Haggerty, K. (2005). 'Policing Fantasy City', in: D. Cooley (eds.), *Re-imagining Policing in Canada*, Toronto: University of Toronto Press: pp. 140-208.

Independent Police Complaints Commission (2011). *Police Complaints: statistics for England and Wales 2010/11*, London.

Jacobson, J. and Saville, E. (1999). *Neighbourhood Warden Schemes: An overview*, Home Office, London (www.homeoffice.gov.uk/rds/prgpdfs/crrs2.pdf, retrieved at 28 December 2012).

Johnston, L. (2003). 'From 'pluralisation' to 'the police extended family': discourses on the governance of community policing in Britain', *International Journal of the Sociology of Law*, 31(3): 185-204.

Johnston, L. (2005). 'From "Community" to Neighbourhood Policing: Police Community Support Officers and the 'Police Extended family' in London', *Journal of Community & Applied Social Psychology*, 15: 241-254.

Johnston, L. (2007). 'Keeping the family together: Police Community Support Officers and the police extended family in London', *Policing and Society*, 17(2): 119-140.

Johnston, L. and Shearing, C. (2003). *Governing Security: Explorations in Policing and Justice*, London: Routledge.

Jones, T. and Newburn, T. (1998), Private Security and Public Policing, Oxford: Clarendon Press.

Jones, T., and Newburn, T. (1999). 'Urban Change and Policing: Mass Private Property Re-considered', *European Journal on Criminal Policy and Research*, 7(2): 225-244.

Jones, T. and Newburn, T. (2002). 'The Transformation of Policing? Understanding Current Trends in Policing Systems', *British Journal of Criminology*, 42: 129-46.

Jones, T. and Newburn, T. (2006a). 'Understanding plural policing', in: T. Jones and T. Newburn (eds.), *Plural policing: A comparative perspective*, London: Routledge: pp. 1-11.

Jones, T. and Newburn, T. (2006b). 'The United Kingdom', in: T. Jones and T. Newburn (eds.), *Plural policing: A comparative perspective*, London: Routledge, pp. 34-44.

Jones, T. and T. Newburn (eds.) (2006c). *Plural policing: A comparative perspective*, London: Routledge.

Jones, T., Steden, R. van and Boutellier, H. (2009). 'Pluralisation of policing in England & Wales and the Netherlands: exploring similarity and difference', *Policing and Society: An International Journal of Research and Policy*, 19(3): 282-299.

Kempa, M., Stenning, P. and Wood, J. (2004). 'Policing communal spaces. A reconfiguration of the 'Mass private property' hypothesis', *British Journal of Criminology*, 44 (4): 562-581.

Koopman, J. (2012). 'Het Nationale Politiebestel: Een Wankel Kaartenhuis', *Tijdschrift voor Constitutioneel Recht*, 3(1): 4-28.

KplusV – Organisatieadvies (2010). *Inzicht in toezicht en handhaving veiligheid en leefbaarheid in de openbare ruimte*, Arnhem: KplusV.

Law Commission of Canada (2001). *In Search of Security: The Roles of Public Police and Private Agencies*, Ottawa.

Law Commission of Canada (2006). *In Search of Security: The Future of Policing in Canada*, Ottawa.

Le Grand, J. and Bartlett, W. (1993). *Quasi-markets and social policy*, Houndmills: MacMillan.

Lindblom, C. (1979). 'Still Muddling, Not Yet Through', *Public Administration Review*, 39(6): 517-526.

Lippert, R. (2012). ''Clean and safe' passage: Business Improvement Districts, urban security modes, and knowledge brokers', *European Urban and Regional Studies*, 19(2): 167-180.

Lippert, R. and O'Connor, D. (2003). 'Security Assemblages: Airport Security, Flexible Work, and Liberal Governance', *Alternatives: Global, Local, Political*, 28: 331-358.

Lithopoulos, S. and Rigakos, G. (2005). 'Neo-liberalism, community, and police regionalization in Canada: A critical empirical analysis', *Policing: An International Journal of Police Strategies & Management*, 28(2): 337-352.

Loader, I. (2000). 'Plural policing and democratic governance', *Social & Legal Studies*, 9(3): 323-345.

Loader, I. and Walker, N. (2007). *Civilizing Security*, Cambridge: Cambridge University Press.

Loveday, B. (2012). 'Police reform in England and Wales: A new dimension in accountability and service delivery in the 21st century', in: N. Fyfe, J. Terpstra and P. Tops (eds.), *Centralizing Forces? Comparative perspectives on contemporary police reform in Northern and Western Europe*, Den Haag: Boom/Eleven, pp. 99-118.

Lyon, D. (2001). *Surveillance society: Monitoring everyday life*, Buckingham: Open University Press.

Manning, P. (2006). 'The United States of America', in: T. Jones and T. Newburn (eds.), *Plural policing: A comparative perspective*, London: Routledge: pp. 98-125.

Manzo, J. (2004). 'The folk devil happens to be our best customer: security officers' orientations to "Youth" in three Canadian shopping malls', *International Journal of the Sociology of Law*, 32: 243-261.

Mawby, R. (2000). 'Tourist' perceptions of security: The risk-fear paradox', *Tourism Economics*, 6(2): 109-121.

Mawby, R. and Wright, A. (2008). 'The police organisation', in: T. Newburn (ed.), *The Handbook of Policing* (second edition). Devon: Willan Publishing: pp. 224-253.

Merritt, J. (2010). 'W(h)ither the PCSO?: Police perceptions of the Police Community Support Officer's role, powers and future directions', *Policing: An International Journal of Police Strategies & Management*, 33(4): 731-749.

Millie, A. and Herrington, V. (2005). 'Bridging the Gap: Understanding Reassurance Policing', *The Howard Journal of Criminal Justice*, 44: 41–56.

Mills, C.W. (1959). *The Sociological Imagination*, London: Oxford University Press.

Ministerie van Justitie (2004). *Particuliere Veiligheidszorg in het Publieke Domein*, Den Haag: Ministerie van Justitie (Brief van de Minister van Justitie aan de Voorzitter van de Tweede Kamer der Staten-Generaal, 7 mei 2004, kenmerk: 5266617/504).

Ministerie van Veiligheid en Justitie (2011). *Circulaire buitengewoon opsporingsambtenaar (kenmerk 5679441/10)*, Den Haag.

Ministerie van Veiligheid en Justitie (2010). *SBV-verkenning Toezicht en Handhaving*, Den Haag.

Ministry of the Interior and Kingdom Relations (2004). *Policing in the Netherlands*, Den Haag.

Mouhanna, C. (2010). 'Rural Policing in France : the End of Genuine Community Policing', in: R. Mawby and R. Yarwood (eds.), *Rural Policing and Policing the Rural. A Constable Countryside?*, Farnham: Ashgate Publishing: pp. 45-57.

Mopas, M. (2005). 'Policing in Vancouver's Downtown Eastside: A Case Study', in: D. Cooley (eds.), *Re-imagining Policing in Canada*, Toronto: University of Toronto Press: pp. 92-139.

Mulone, M. (2012). 'When Private and Public Policing Merge: Thoughts on Commercial Policing', *Social Justice*, 38 (1-2).

Murphy, C., and Clarke. C. (2005). 'A Study of Policing and Security in Two Canadian Communities', in: D. Cooley, (eds.), *Re-imagining Policing in Canada*, Toronto: University of Toronto Press: pp. 209-259.

Neighbourhood Renewal Unit (2002). *Neighbourhood and Street Wardens' Programme*, London.

Neighbourhood Renewal Unit (2004). *Research Report 8: Neighbourhood Wardens Scheme Evaluation* ODPM, London. (www.crimereduction.gov.uk/wardens32.htm, retrieved at 28 December 2012).

Nelken, D. (1994). 'Whom can you Trust? The Future of Comparative Criminology', in: D. Nelken (eds.), *The Futures of Criminology*, London: Sage Publications Limited: pp. 220-243.

Nelken, D. (2002). 'Comparing Criminal Justice', in: M. Maguire, R. Morgan, and R. Reiner (eds.), *The Oxford Handbook of Criminology* (third revised edition), Oxford: Oxford University Press: pp. 175-202.

Neuhofer, H. (1998). *Gemeinderecht. Organisation und Aufgaben der Gemeinden in Österreich*, Wenen/New York: Springer.

Newburn, T. (2001). 'The commodification of policing: security networks in the late modern city', *Urban Studies*, 38(5-6): 829-848.

Newburn, T. and Sparks, R. (2004). 'Criminal justice and political cultures', in: T. Newburn and R. Sparks (eds.), *Criminal justice and political cultures*, Cullompton: Willan: pp. 1-15.

Newman, J. (2001). *Modernizing governance: New Labour, policy and society*, London: Sage.

Noaks, L. (2000). 'Private cops on the block: A review of the role of private security in residential communities', *Policing and Society*, 10(2): 143-61.

Noaks, L. (2008). 'Private and public Policing in the UK: a citizen perspective on partnership', *Policing and Society*, 18(2): 156-168.

Norris, C. and McCahill, M. (2008). 'CCTV: Beyond Penal Modernism?', *British Journal of Criminology*, 46(1): 97-118.

OACP (Ontario Association of Chiefs of Police) (2010). *Report on Special Constables in Ontario. A White Paper*. Ottawa.

O'Connor, C. (2008). 'Citizen attitudes toward the police in Canada', *Policing: An International Journal of Police Strategies and Management*, 31(4): 578-595.

OPP (Ontario Provincial Police) (2011). *Strategic Plan 2011-2013*, Ottawa.

Osborne, D. and Gaebler, T. (1992). *Reinventing government*, New York: Plume.

Pakes, F. (2005). 'Penalization and retreat: The changing face of Dutch criminal justice', *Criminal Justice*, 5(2): 145-161.

Pakes, F. (2006). 'The ebb and flow of criminal justice in the Netherlands', *International Journal of the Sociology of Law*, 34(4): 141-156.

Paskell, C. (2007). ''Plastic Police' Or 'Community Support'? : The Role of Police Community Support Officers Within Low-Income Neighbourhoods', *European Urban and Regional Studies*, 14(4): 349-361.

Pollitt, C. (1993). *Managerialism and the public services* (2nd rev. edition). Oxford: Blackwell.

Pollitt, C. (1998). 'Managerialism Revisited', in: G. Peters and D. Savoie, *Taking Stock: Assessing Public Sector Reforms*, Montreal: McGill-Queen's University Press.

Ponsaers, P., Enhus E., and Hutsebaut, F. (eds.) (2006). *Het kerntakendebat continued*, Cahiers politiestudies, Brussels: Politeia.

Punch, M. and Naylor, T. (1973). 'The police: a social service', *New Society*, 17(554): 358-361.

Reiner, R. (2010). *The Politics of the Police* (fourth edition), Oxford University Press, Oxford.

Reuss-Ianni, E. (1983). *Two Cultures of Policing: Street Cops and Management Cops*, New Brunswick: Transaction Publishers.

Rigakos, G. (2002). *The New Parapolice: Risk Markets and Commodified Social Control*, Toronto: University of Toronto Press.

Rigakos, G. (2011). *The Downtown Yonge BIA Safety and Security Tracking Study*, Carleton: Carleton University.

Rigakos, G. and Greener, D. (2000). 'Bubbles of Governance: Private Policing and the Law in Canada', *Canadian Journal of Law and Society*, 15(1): 145-185.

Rigakos, G. and Leung, C. (2006). 'Canada', in: T. Jones and T. Newburn (eds.), *Plural policing: A comparative perspective*, London: Routledge: pp. 126-138.

Savage, S. (2007). *Police Reform. Forces For Change*, Oxford: Oxford University Press.

Scanlon, K. (2006). *Neighbourhood wardens: the activity pattern in one English City*, Ljubljana: ENHR conference.

Schuilenburg, M. (2012). *Orde in veiligheid. Een dynamisch perspectief*, Den Haag: Boom Lemma.

Scott, I. (2011). *Development of Civilian Oversight of the Police in Ontario*, Toronto: Ontario's Special Investigations Unit.

Security Industry Authority (2010). *Get Licensed, SIA licensing criteria*, Liverpool.

Shearing, C. and Stenning, P. (1983). 'Private security: implications for social control', *Social Problems*, 30(5): 493-506.

Sleiman, M. and Lippert, R. (2010). 'Downtown ambassadors, police relations and 'clean and safe' security', *Policing & Society*, 20(3): 316-335.

Smeets, S. (2008). 'New uniforms of local governance of security in Belgium', in: L. Cachet, P. Ponsaers et al. (eds.), *Governance of Security in the Netherlands and Belgium*, Den Haag: Boom Juridische uitgevers: pp. 177-196.

Social Exclusion Unit (1999). *Report of Policy Action Team 6 on Neighbourhood Wardens*, London: Cabinet Office.

Statistics Canada (2010), *Police Resources in Canada*, Canadian Centre for Justice Statistics.

Steden, R. van (2007). *Privatizing policing: Describing and explaining the growth of private security*, Den Haag: Boom Juridische uitgevers.

Steden, R. van (2009). 'De pretparksamenleving. Een wereld van veilig vertier', in: H. Boutellier, N. Boonstra and M. Ham (eds.), *Omstreden Ruimte. Over de organisatie van spontaniteit en veiligheid*, Amsterdam: Van Gennep: pp. 15-31.

Steden, R. van (2012). *Veelvormig en versnipperd: gemeentelijke toezichthouders en handhavers in het publieke domein*, Den Haag: SMVP.

Steden, R. van and Bron, E. (2012) *Gemeentelijke handhavers in Amsterdam: een onderzoek naar hun werk op straat*, Den Haag: Boom-Lemma.

Steden, R. van and Jones, T. (2008). 'Straatcoaches in Slotervaart. Enige kanttekeningen bij het idee van een 'overheid op afstand'', in: *Tijdschrift voor Veiligheid*, 7(4): 20-29.

Steden, R. van en Waard, J. de (2013). 'Acting like chameleons: On the MacDonaldization of private security', *Security Journal* (forthcoming).

Stenning, P. (2009). 'Governance and Accountability in a Plural Policing Environment – The Story so Far', *Policing*, 3(1): 22-33.

Stolzlechner, H. and Horvath, T. (2009). 'Sicherheitsverwaltung und Privatwirtschaft', *SIAK-Journal. Zeitschrift für Polizeiwissenschaft und polizeilicher Praxis*, 4: 67-81.

Swaan, A. de (1982). *De mens is de mens een zorg. Opstellen 1971-1981*, Amsterdam: Meulenhof.

Terpstra, J. (2002). *Sturing van politie en politiewerk. Een verkennend onderzoek tegen de achtergrond van een veranderende sturingscontext en sturingsstijl*, Zeist: Kerckebosch.

Terpstra, J. (2004). 'Lokale inbedding van de Nederlandse politie: stand van zaken en overzicht', in: F. Vlek, K. Bangma, K. Loef en E. Muller (eds.), *Uit balans: politie en bestel in de knel. State-of-the-art van kennis en inzichten*, Zeist/Apeldoorn: Kerckebosch/CP&W: pp. 59-80.

Terpstra, J. (2008). *Wijkagenten en hun dagelijks werk: een onderzoek naar de uitvoering van gebiedsgebonden politiewerk*, Den Haag: Reed Business.

Terpstra, J. (2010a). *Het Veiligheidscomplex. Ontwikkelingen, strategieën en verantwoordelijkheden in de veiligheidszorg*, Den Haag: Boom Juridische uitgevers.

Terpstra, J. (2010b). *De maatschappelijke opdracht van de politie. Over identiteit en kernelementen van politiewerk*, Den Haag: Boom Juridische uitgevers.

Terpstra, J. (2011). 'Regulering in een hybride veiligheidszorg. Over de bewaking van een publiek goed in een deels geprivatiseerd bestel', *Tijdschrift voor Veiligheid*, 10(4): 41-58

Terpstra, J. (2012a). 'Particuliere beveiligers als publieke handhavers. De inzet van private boa's door gemeenten', *Justitiële Verkenningen*, 38(8): 35-50.

Terpstra, J. (2012b). 'The Warning and Advisory Task of the Police: Forging a Link between Police Information and Multi-Agency Partnerships', *Policing*, 6(1): 67-75.

Terpstra, J. (2013). 'Towards a national police in the Netherlands – backgrounds of a radical police reform', in: N. Fyfe, J. Terpstra and P. Tops (eds.), *Centralizing Forces? Comparative perspectives on contemporary police reform in Northern and Western Europe*, The Hague: Boom Eleven: pp. 137-156.

Terpstra, J. and Gunther Moor, L. (2012). 'Nationale politie. Kanttekeningen tegen de stroom in', *Nederlands Juristenblad*, 87(7): 451-457.

Terpstra, J. and Havinga, T. (2005). 'Gemeenten, boetes en kleine ergernissen', *Justitiële Verkenningen*, 31(6): 10-22.

Terpstra, J. and Kouwenhoven, R. (2004). *Samenwerking en netwerken in de lokale veiligheidszorg*, Zeist: Kerckebosch.

Terpstra, J. Gunther Moor, L. and Stokkom, B. van (2010). 'De kerntakendiscussie in Nederland. Retoriek en realiteit', in: B. van Stokkom, J. Terpstra and L. Gunther Moor (et al.) (eds.), *De politie en haar opdracht. De kerntakendiscussie voorbij*, Antwerpen: Maklu: pp. 25-50.

Terpstra, J. and Trommel, W. (2006). *Het Nieuwe Bedrijfsmatig Denken bij de Politie. Een analyse van een culturele formatie in ontwikkeling*, Den Haag: Elsevier.

Terpstra, J. and Trommel, W. (2009). 'Police, managerialization and presentational strategies', *Policing: An International Journal of Police Strategies & Management*, 32(1): 128-143.

Terpstra, J. and Vijver, K. van der (2005). 'Het Nederlandse politiebestel en de druk tot centralisatie', *Tijdschrift voor Criminologie*, 47(4): 335-344.

Torre-Eilert, T. van der, Bergsma, H. and Duin, M. van (2010). *Lokale politiek over politie*, Apeldoorn: Politie & Wetenschap.

Verwee, I. (2009). 'Wat doet de politie? Onderzoek naar de dagelijkse politiepraktijk', *Cahiers Politiestudies*, 4(14): 37-67.

Waarden, F. van (2006). 'Werk in een wantrouwende wereld: omvang en oorzaken van een uitdijende controle-industrie', *Beleid en Maatschappij*, 33 (4): 232-251.

Wakefield, A. (2003). *Selling Security: The Private Policing of Public Space*, Cullompton: Willan.

Wakefield, A. (2005). 'The Public Surveillance Functions of Private Security', *Surveillance & Society*, 2 (4): 529-545.

Wakefield, A. (2006). 'The Security Officer', in: M. Gill (eds.), *The Handbook of Security*, Houndmills Palgrave: pp. 383-407.

Wenda, G. (2011a). 'Gemeindesicherheitswachen. Partner für Sicherheit in den Gemeinden', *Kommunal*, 12: 24-25.

Wenda, G. (2011b). 'Gemeindesicherheitswachen. Partner der Bundespolizei', *Öffentliche Sicherheit*, 11-12: 10-14.

Wenda, G. (2013). 'Municipal police in Austria: History, status quo and future', in: *Public Safety, Legal and Organizational Functioning of Municipal Police in Europe*, Cracow (forthcoming).

White, A. (2010). *The Politics of Private Security: Regulation, Reform and Re-legitimation*, Palgrave Macmillan.

White, A. and Gill, M. (2013). 'The Transformation of Policing: From Ratios to Rationalities', *British Journal of Criminology*, 53(1): 74-93.

White, A., and Smith, M. (2009). *The Security Industry Authority, A Baseline Review*, Sheffield: The University of Sheffield.

Wood, J. and Shearing, C. (2007). *Imagining security*, Cullompton: Willan.

Zedner, L. (2003). 'Too much security?', *International Journal of the Sociology of Law*, 31(3): 135-184.

Zedner, L. (2006). 'Policing before and after the police: The historical antecedents of contemporary crime control', *British Journal of Criminology,* 46(1): 78-96.